Jefferson's Nightmare

The Domination of the World Financial System

William O. Joseph

Greenstone Creative

Bigfork, Montana

Greenstone Creative Inc.
202 N. Crestview Terrace
Bigfork, MT 59911
www.JeffersonsNightmare.com

Jefferson's Nightmare:
The Domination of the World Financial System

ISBN 978-0-692-63025-9

This book is dedicated to the memory

of my dear friend and colleague,

Janet Morrow

Janet's favorite quote:

*"If you want to change the world,
you have to change the metaphor"*

Joseph Campbell

CONTENTS

ACKNOWLEDGMENTS

First and foremost, this book is the result of a nearly 30 year conversation with my wife, Marshelle, for which nothing in writing could ever adequately convey my deepest gratitude. No man ever had a more trustworthy and steadfast companion on the quest for truth and meaning.

Secondly, thanks to my son AJ Joseph for his wisdom, marketing knowledge and graphic skills.

Thanks to my dear friend and fellow writer, P.G. Lengsfelder for his insights. Thanks to Jasmine Booker, Marcus Grail, Matt Hicks, Ben and Gillian McCord, Geffen Rothe and Patricia Winslow for their friendship and advice.

The original manuscript turned into two different books. Not to worry my friends, volume two is on the way.

Cover design was produced by Jason Seiler, my favorite portrait artist. Many thanks Jason. See: www.jasonseiler.com

INTRODUCTION

The citizen's of our great country are haunted by a specter of uncertainty. James Carville, of whom I have never been particularly fond, demonstrated a knack for getting directly to the point when, during the 1991 presidential campaign, he coined the phrase:

"It's the economy, stupid!"

It's the economy, stupid, because nothing hits us where we live quite so powerfully as how hard we must work to make a living for our families. Those who have been in the workforce for decades and have experienced the carnage of a continually expanding and contracting economy, want answers to some serious questions. Why don't we have an inherently stable economy? Why can't we have faith that the carefully stored fruits of our labor from previous decades will be still be available when, in our old age, we need to rely on them? Why are the economic forces at work in our world so volatile?

There are hoards of pundits with a variety of ideas about the what the most pressing economic issues are. They all manipulate carefully chosen statistics to support conflicting points of view. We are told unemployment is only 5% and the economy is gaining strength day by day. People who have been looking for work for a long time tell a different story. We seem to be doomed to argue endlessly over choosing the right leader to lead a system which has been undergoing gradual structural failure since

World War I. Some say, our biggest problem is too many people who ***don't*** want to work. In my view, a much bigger problem is, there are too many people who ***do*** want to work, but can't find a job opportunity that provides a living wage. Add the specter of uncertainty that an opportunity to earn a living might not even continue to exist and you have the makings of Jefferson's Nightmare.

There is a growing sense among the population that something is not quite right with our financial system. Those of us, who were in business during the 1990's, can remember being faced with so much economic opportunity we couldn't find enough people to hire. That's clearly no longer the case. The question bubbling away in the background is:

Why do economic boom and bust cycles exist?

I was born in the United States and grew up here. The ideas in this book represent the opinion of a white middle class American. I make no apology for that. I'm just a regular guy trying to make my way in the country I love. This book is not intended to be a scholarly work and I'm not going to try to prove to you what I'm saying. I'd rather you look at the ideas in this book and tell me how they can be improved and expanded upon. This book is about how it feels to be a middle class American senior in 2016. You will need to make up your own mind whether or not to embrace those feelings and opinions.

My attitude reflects the experiences I have collected while unknowingly participating in the degradation of the American Dream. Sometimes, the most difficult things to see clearly are the things we take for granted. The American Dream is not what it was in Jefferson's day. The words we use to describe it are the same, but the meanings have changed.

When, as a child, I said, "I'm proud to be an American," I meant I was proud we won World War II and that we, the United States of America, were number one in the world. The leader of the Allies. We were the good guys. My heroes were, Zorro, Roy Rogers, Superman and Vic Morrow who starred in the TV show "Combat." I was elated as they triumphed over evil by being fair and honest and shooting more accurately than the bad guys. Roy never shot anyone between the eyes, or splattered brains on the wall. He shot the gun out of their hand and trundled them off to jail. I was thrilled to participate, as we stood against overwhelming odds for truth, justice and the American Way. Life was much simpler in the fifties. There were the white hats and the black hats and the white hats always won. The American Dream has acquired a little tarnish since then.

Nearly 60 years later, when I say, "I'm proud to be an American," I have to think deeply about what that really means to me. Am I proud of the impression the American government leaves behind as it stumbles through world affairs? No, not at all. I believe the actions of our government continually misrepresent the character and intent of the American people. In the fifties and early sixties I thought the government was supposed to *be* the character and intent of the American people. That's what they taught us in school. Am I proud of the morality exhibited by our business leaders as they lay waste to the international economic landscape in pursuit of personal economic glorification? Definitely not.

What does make me proud to be an American requires some explanation. I have always admired Thomas Jefferson. He was an author, an architect, an inventor, a horticulturist and a politician. In 1776 he penned,

"We hold these truths to be self evident, that all men are created equal, that they are endowed by their creator with certain unalienable rights, that among these are life, liberty and the pursuit of happiness."

He was basing our declaration of independence from the British Aristocracy upon a right to self determination that was not granted by royalty, the church or the privileged few. He was declaring that the rights he outlined in the Declaration of Independence were built into the being of every free man by his creator. He was claiming that no matter what happens, those rights are inherently ours and cannot be taken from us.

We fought against the British Crown because the aristocracy felt they were entitled to too large a piece of the American economic pie. When economic forces outside of us demand so much of our ability to produce that we cannot provide for ourselves and our families without borrowing from and becoming indebted to them—well, that's the stuff revolutions are made of. When someone willfully restricts access to the rights we hold so dear, something needs to change, one way or the other.

Let's not be naive about the cultural climate of Jefferson's day. When he wrote "All men are created equal," the prevailing sentiment of his day was that all landed white men are created equal. At the same time we fought against the British Crown to secure our freedom from the aristocracy, we also repressed women, Native Americans and newly kidnapped Africans. Jefferson was a plantation owner in Virginia. That economy was built on the backs of slave labor. He couldn't continue to be a plantation owner without being a slave owner at the same time. We all must live in the context of our time.

Was Jefferson simply accepting the cultural restrictions of his day? Some light is shed on that question by what he wrote in a preliminary draft of the Constitution of the State of Virginia in 1783:

"The General assembly shall not have the power to permit the introduction of any more slaves to reside in this state, or the continuance of slavery beyond the generation which shall be living on the 31st day of December, 1800; all persons born after that day being hereby declared free."

Jefferson was actively campaigning for an end to the system upon which his own fortune depended. In my view, he had a vision of what America could become. He was consciously planting a seed of possibility that could grow into a great egalitarian society of the future. Even though the subjugation of human beings was still condoned in the United States, Jefferson was reaching for a higher cultural ideal. We have struggled for over two centuries to realize that vision. We are still struggling to say definitively that the phrase, "All men are created equal," includes all men and all women regardless of their race, creed or color.

Jefferson believed that liberty, the right to self determination, was the foundation stone upon which the great republic would be built. He described the ideal American citizen as being "the yeoman farmer." The yeoman farmer owned his land, free and clear, having wrested it out of the primeval forest. By virtue of the concentrated effort of himself and his family unit, he was self sufficient and was able to produce a surplus beyond what his family consumed. He was a rifleman, capable of defending himself, his family and his community if the need arose. He owed no man save for his pledge to share life, liberty and the pursuit of happiness with his fellow citizens. He was the defender of freedom. The American ideal.

What makes me proud to be an American is our collective commitment to the ideal of freedom. Despite what has actually happened in the last 240 years, we still carry that commitment in our hearts and minds. It's in our DNA. In America we haven't actually achieved the level of freedom we have stood for and given so many lives to defend. That doesn't mean it's not possible. In order to pursue the concept of real freedom for all, we will need to re-define what it really means. While thinking we were operating the American dream of home ownership, we traded our freedom for a pile of debt. As the following chapters will show, the great majority of us will never actually own anything. It all belongs to the bank. Most of us are just renters, no matter what it says on the title.

Over the last 60 years, we have slowly allowed the money masters to acquire a level of control over all of us that is unprecedented in the history of humanity. So slowly that we didn't really notice, we find ourselves cocooned in a financial system that does not stand for the prosperity of the people. We also find ourselves governed by a political system that exists to pander to the Aristocracy of Capital. Both our political system and our financial system, stand for the rights of the Aristocracy of Capital first and the rights of the people at some time in the future. Maybe. One of the threads of this story is how I came to understand that in my own life.

I don't really want to join the ranks of the conspiracy theorists. However, I do see an event cascade assembling in the background of current events that could have dire consequences if we don't act decisively to change our collective behavior. As I watch the world's political and financial news unfold, I am certain that we need to pay more attention to what's behind what's happening on the surface. We should be very concerned about what the people who are really in power are doing. More than that, we should be very concerned about what we all believe is normal.

Those who can see what is actually going on in the world have a sacred responsibility to come forward and point out, not only where we are, but where we could go from here. Jefferson's deepest fear was that despite the commitment of its people, despite all the lives lost in the defense of freedom, that the ideals upon which the United States of America was founded would slowly be corrupted from within. We are going to take a good hard look at the degree to which that has already happened. Then we'll talk about what to do. My conclusions live outside of the cultural box we have allowed ourselves to be confined in. I hope they will be useful in helping us rise to the challenge of waking from Jefferson's Nightmare.

William O. Joseph
2016

PART I

The Dominators

CHAPTER ONE

Jefferson's Nightmare

Thomas Jefferson was deeply engaged in a battle with the financial system of his day. Few people are aware that the third president of the United States was 100,000 dollars in debt when he died in 1826. That may not sound like a lot of money in modern terms until we realize that 100,000 dollars in 1826 American currency is equal to 2.5 million dollars today. That *is* a lot of money! It also means that today's dollar is worth **25 *times less*** than it was in Jefferson's day. A statistic like that should strike fear in our hearts and cause us to protest, but it doesn't. The reason it doesn't, is that we haven't been taught what it really means. A spell has been cast upon us by the warlocks of the financial world. That spell whispers in our ears:

"The loss of the value of your money is a naturally occurring phenomenon, there is nothing to worry about, everything will adjust by itself."

What the steady and gradual loss of the value of our currency really means is that the purchasing power and real value of the money you use every day is being confiscated by someone for their own personal gain. How is that possible? Who would do such a thing? That, is the subject of this book. Jefferson understood very well what was behind the loss of value of our currency. It haunted his dreams. He summarized his recurring nightmare when he wrote:

"If the American People ever allow private banks to control the issue of currency, first by inflation, then by deflation, the banks and corporations that will grow up around them will deprive the people of all property until their children wake up homeless on the continent their fathers conquered."

Why would the American people ever allow private banks to control the issuance of our currency? Isn't that a role left to our government? We, the people, would allow that if we didn't know it was happening. We would allow it if we didn't understand why it was happening. The workings of the financial world are intentionally complex. That is why we haven't understood en masse what is really happening to us.

I'm not an economist, I'm just a regular guy who works for a living. I'm going to do my best to describe the elements of Jefferson's Nightmare in the same way your neighbor would tell you the story of being swindled out of his life savings by a con man. I want as many people as possible to understand what has been done to the American Dream and why. We will run through the elements of Jefferson's Nightmare quickly to establish the concept. Then we'll go back for a detailed look at how this system evolved.

The Elements of Jefferson's Nightmare

<u>**Controlling The Issue of Currency:**</u> We have been taught that our banks collect our deposits and then extend credit to us

by loaning that money back to those who can qualify to take on debt. Our banks can loan us money because they are the ones who have it, right? Not exactly. Our banks are actually allowed to loan out ninety percent of the amount of money we have deposited with them. They are also allowed to say they still have it in our accounts. How can our money be in two places at once? Isn't that some kind of fundamental fraud?

When a bank loans out our money while claiming they still have in on deposit, the bank is actually creating money in the form of credit or debt. That is what Jefferson meant by allowing private banks to issue currency. Money created from nothing is offered to us in the form of car loans, home mortgages, credit cards and other kinds of retail and corporate debt we take on. In our modern world, we are taught that our credit rating is one of our most important assets. Without a good credit rating we will not be able to borrow the money we need to buy a house or a car or whatever else our heart desires. Our system is built upon what is now a rock solid assumption:

Working people cannot earn enough to be debt free citizens. Working people do not possess an abundance of money and must borrow from those who do in order to enjoy a reasonable standard of living.

That's the assumption we live under because, in our present reality, it has come true. Actually, it's been true for a very long time. There is a series of questions we should be asking—Why can't the labor of a family unit provide a reasonable debt free standard of living? Why must we borrow from those who have money? How did the people with vast amounts of capital become the ones who have money to lend while the rest of us do not?

The rate at which new money is created as credit is controlled by another private bank known as the United States Federal Reserve. If you are one of the few people left on the planet that didn't know the United States Federal Reserve is a privately held bank and not a government entity, well then, surprise, surprise!

The "Fed," as it is known, possesses the gas pedal of the economy and attempts to control the rate at which new money is created as credit. Unfortunately Fed policy must compete with the effects generated by Wall Street market riggers for domination of the control panel. We'll explore how that works in later chapters.

You've all heard the negative tone of voice that is used when our financial commentators declare, "Yeah, they are printing money again." To grasp that concept we'll go back to a time when paper money was backed by gold. Very simply and quickly—Let's say it's 1850 and you have inherited a working gold mine from your uncle who was a prospector.

You decide to go into the banking business. You buy a two room storefront on the main street of your little town. In one room you place a big pile of gold. You are more than a little stingy and don't want to let go of the physical gold. When you investigated the banking business you discovered that the problem of keeping the gold on hand had already been solved.

Rather than loaning out the physical gold, other banks were printing pieces of paper called bank notes. Each bank note says that it can be redeemed for gold at any time. Everyone knows that gold is heavy and awkward to carry about. Walking around with a pocket full of lightweight paper notes of equivalent value is much more appealing. So, you put a printing press in the basement and fill the second room in your bank with one hundred thousand bank notes. You tell the people that the one hundred thousand pieces of paper equal one hundred thousand shares of the gold in the other room.

You tell the people in your town that starting next Monday they can come to your bank and borrow those pieces of paper, each one, representing a hundred thousandth share of the gold. You convince them that they can trade freely with those pieces of paper. You tell them they can come back and exchange their pieces of paper for real gold at any time. But you suspect that few people will, because gold is heavy and awkward to carry about.

Monday comes and you open the loan window. People are lining up to borrow your gold certificates, counting on their previously declared value of a one hundred thousandth share of the gold. Over the weekend you have printed an additional one hundred thousand pieces of paper in anticipation of the next shipment of gold which has not yet arrived from your gold mine.

As the original one hundred thousand pieces of paper are being loaned out the front window, your staff is bringing another one hundred thousand pieces of paper up from the basement, where the presses are. You plan to store them until the next shipment of gold arrives from the mine. Then a messenger arrives from the mine to tell you there has been an accident and the next gold shipment will be delayed. As your customers line up to borrow your bank notes, you realize, none of them know you have printed another one hundred thousand pieces of paper. In that moment something truly incredible dawns upon you:

Once you have loaned out the first hundred thousand pieces of paper, you can continue to loan out the second hundred thousand at face value and nobody will be the wiser.

The people are counting on the previously declared value of each of your bank notes. But, by loaning out the second hundred thousand pieces of paper, you have cut the value of each piece of previously printed paper by half and nobody knows it has happened. You will profit enormously from loan payments on the second hundred thousand bank notes that in essence are not backed by your gold and that cost you only the price of paper and ink to create.

That is how currency is issued by banks in the modern world. In this example, the bank has robbed the people of half the value of their currency without them even knowing about the theft. That is how the purchasing power and real value of your money can be confiscated by someone without your knowledge or permission. The foregoing story is a highly simplified description of how printing money causes existing money to lose its value. This is why in a nutshell, one dollar in Jefferson's day is only worth 4 cents today. We will go into the history of the process a little more deeply in Chapter Four.

We don't really print money anymore, except to replace worn out bills. There is no longer any gold in the bank that you can exchange your paper for. Today, money is created electronically as debt. When you go to the bank to take out your car loan, they don't give you cash or gold. They give you a piece of paper that says it is worth so many other pieces of paper. You take that piece of paper to the car dealer and exchange it for the car. Then, the payments begin.

The effect on the real value of your existing money is the same whether it is created electronically or as paper. Creating money as credit or debt, inflates the money supply and makes your money worth less over time. The people who use the fraudulent pieces of paper you printed, as money, don't exactly understand what has been done to them.

However, over time the people will sense the change in the value of their money because they can tell they are constantly having to work harder than before, to earn more money, to acquire the same amount of goods as before. Those who can, adjust by raising the price of their labor or the price of the goods they manufacture. Those who live on fixed salaries will simply try to cope by accepting a steadily declining standard of living. Creating money as credit or debt causes prices to rise. When prices rise at an accelerating rate, we call that inflation.

Inflation: There are thousands of retail banks, credit card companies, finance companies and mortgage lenders. They are all participating in the creation of money as credit. It's kind of like drug dealing. Once your bank has loaned out ninety percent of the money you put on deposit, it can borrow more fake money from the Federal Reserve. Your bank will then mark up the interest on that money and loan to you. The Federal Reserve creates great gobs of money out of nothing in the form of commercial credit. That commercial credit descends through the ranks of the national dealers to the regional dealers to the local dealers and finally to you in the form of retail credit.

The next loan you take out includes a financial cut for each and every dealer through which the drugs, er—credit, have passed. As in drug dealing, the higher a dealer is on the food chain, the more money they make by volume. They are motivated to loan money to you, because by creating money as credit, they make enormous amounts of it on their own behalf.

We are talking about what is euphemistically referred to, by economists, as *The Business Cycle.* As Jefferson outlined, the business cycle has an inflationary part and a deflationary part. During the inflationary part of the cycle, all those lenders and creators of money as credit, are spinning up the RPM's of the credit machine. To make the economy go faster, the lenders have eased the requirements under which they are willing to loan you their printed money. They have also temporarily lowered the interest rate they are charging to make their loans more affordable. People are borrowing faster and faster. The borrowed money is being used to buy homes, cars, appliances, furniture and everything else that can be produced. The borrowed money is fueling economic expansion. Everyone has a job and the factories are singing. Everyone is making money. But, prices are also rising at a rapid rate.

Here is the story of how the business cycle affected Harry Homeowner and his family.

Harry and his wife, Tina, had been scrimping and saving for years to accumulate enough money to put 20% down on their first California home in 1996. It was a modest affair, but all Harry could afford on his salary as a junior project manager for a local construction company. Tina had decided to dedicate her life to her children by being a stay at home mom. The economy had recently recovered from something called "recession" and the lenders were once again offering attractive real estate loans. That was good news for Harry since the new vitality in home lending was stimulating residential construction and creating more work for his company. It was also creating more and more sales to subcontractors and suppliers of everything needed to build a home. The concrete people, the carpenters, the lumber yard, and the roofers were all doing well. Nearly everyone was employed and working people were starting to feel more prosperous.

Working people everywhere were starting to feel more confident that there would continue to be an abundance of money in the near future. They demonstrated their confidence not only by buying new homes, but also by purchasing new cars, furniture and clothing. They ate out more often.

Harry was moving up the corporate ladder. He was handling more home building projects than ever before. The boss gave him a raise in the form of a performance bonus. The more homes he built, the more money he would make. He was starting to dream about that ski boat he had always wanted. It would be a fun way to spend time with the family and a good way to lower the increasing stress he was feeling at work.

The money that had been created as credit to buy all the new homes being built was trickling down into every facet of the local community. The businesses that supplied materials and services directly to the construction industry were doing well. The restaurant guy, the real estate agent, the appraiser, the insurance salesman, the car dealership and the home supply store were all making money too. Because of the substantial amounts of interest being charged on all the new home mortgages they created, local, regional and national lenders were literally rolling in cash. The American Dream was working the way it was supposed to. Sort of.

However, because so much money was being created as debt, the amount of money in circulation was increasing rapidly. As a result, the people's money was gradually losing its value. All the businesses that supplied labor and materials to the construction industry sensed the change and began to raise their prices to compensate. Gradually home prices started to increase as well.

Harry, being in the construction business himself, paid attention to such things. After owning their first home for six years, Harry and Tina noticed that the price they could sell it for had risen substantially. As a bonus, the amount they owed on their home had actually decreased, if only slightly. The spread between the sales price of their home and the amount they owed on it meant that Harry and Tina's net worth was increasing month by month, at least on paper.

The family was growing and soon the kids would need to have their own bedrooms. If Harry and Tina sold after owning their current home for only six years, they would walk away with 150,000 dollars in equity. They both knew that due to the fact that prices for everything were rising, there was no other way for them to save so much money. Being in the building business, both Harry and his wife understood houses and knew just what kind of home they wanted next. If they invested wisely they could apply a 20% down payment of 100,000 to the purchase of a brand new 1/2 million dollar home and put 50,000 dollars in the bank as well. It would be criminally stupid not to take advantage of this opportunity. So in 2001 that is exactly what they did.

Living in their new home and having 50,000 dollars in the bank made them feel even more prosperous. The future of Harry's business looked bright, so Harry and Tina spent 15,000 on new blinds, drapes and furniture. Once they got over spending that much money on home improvements it was easy to justify buying the ski boat for another 15,000 dollars. Boating was something they could all do together. The boat would bring them closer as a family.

They still had a 20,000 dollar cushion left in the bank. The real estate lenders were still lending and homes were still selling. Harry was busy and life was good. Home prices kept rising. Harry had been working at capacity for some time now and his salary had gone up a little, but he could only work so hard. He was making all he could expect to make in his current position. He continued to work hard in the home building business for the next 5 years.

In thinking about his situation, Harry realized that he and Tina had never made so much money so fast as they had in buying and selling the last house. They had only been in the new house for 5 years, but if they sold now they could step up once again and parlay their investment into a really nice 750,000 dollar dream home. If they played their cards right, the appreciation they could make on the bigger home would be enormous. In the meantime, every family member would have their own bedroom suite and the third garage would allow them to keep the boat indoors.

After the kids were grown and gone and it came time to stop working, they would be able to sell the dream home and walk away with enough capital to establish their retirement. They thought it over. Their current loan was for 400,000 dollars. If they sold now they could buy the 750,000 dollar house, and put 250,000 down. The new mortgage of 500,000 was a lot, but everyone knows, you have to spend money to make money.

In 2002 the local mortgage company made their decision easier. They told Harry and Tina they could qualify for a subprime loan for the new home on very reasonable terms. For the first five years, the payments would be drastically reduced by a very low interest rate. During the first five years, their mortgage payments, on the much more expensive home, would actually stay about the same as they were now. After five years, the mortgage interest rate would adjust to whatever the prime interest rate was at the time plus two additional percentage points. If the payments grew uncomfortable in five years, they could always sell again or refinance.

Their experience had shown them that they only needed to hold a home for a five year period to acquire a substantial profit. So, Harry and Tina borrowed the absolute limit they could afford. The unfortunate part of this story is that a significant percentage of the American population were doing the same thing at various economic levels. Home flipping had become a national craze, not only in the United States, but around the world. The craze was being fueled by money created from nothing as credit.

Aging couples were selling the large homes they had acquired at the peak of their earning years and using their equity to pay cash for smaller retirement properties. People in Harry's income bracket were buying those homes and each successive tier of income earners were moving up. Everyone was taking advantage of sub-prime financing and borrowing all their incomes could service at the peak of the credit binge.

Harry and Tina had nice furniture, which they had purchased for the previous home, and so spent very little decorating the new dream house. They decided to buckle down and concentrate on reducing their debts in preparation for the increased expenses they would face when their new loan adjusted in five years. The general population had also taken on as much debt as it could in an attempt to take advantage of appreciating home prices. Borrowing slowed dramatically as the credit binge peaked.

The rapid appreciation of the value of our homes and other assets is what Jefferson meant by "*First by inflation.*" Inflation is fueled by money created as easy credit. Debt and credit are the same thing. Credit is what the lender extends to you, debt is the obligation you take on when you sign the loan papers. The home price appreciation Harry and Tina took advantage of was not a naturally occurring event. It was artificially induced by the masters of our financial system through the creation of money as debt. Easy credit is the gas pedal of the economy. The money masters love easy credit because they make billions of dollars in interest by offering it. But easy credit has its limits. When borrowing finally peaks, and it always does, the next part of the cycle begins.

Deflation: The economy had adjusted to a condition of abundant financial growth based upon borrowed money. During the credit binge, every small business that could, hired more people and invested in more equipment to take advantage of the increase in sales that was happening during the boom years. Overall retail debt had increased ten-fold in the last decade. Like Harry and Tina, everyone slowly realized they had signed up for all of the debt they could possibly pay the payments on. Everyone who had borrowed at that level had no choice but to stop borrowing and stop buying at the same rate as before. It was time to fully appreciate what they had and concentrate on enjoying it as much as possible.

Somehow, the pleasure Harry and Tina derived from living in the really big dream home faded and began to be overshadowed by worry. Harry was still upbeat about the future but Tina was worried that they had over-extended themselves. Everyone had reached their absolute credit limit around the same time. When all borrowers stop borrowing, an economy, fueled by money created as debt, cannot continue to expand and begins to contract immediately.

Home sales slowed. The money that trickled down into all of the other businesses from the boom in lending and construction began to dry up. Local businesses started passing out pink slips. Spending on sub-contractors and materials was reduced. More and more people that had previously enjoyed gainful employment were looking for work.

In 2006 home prices leveled off. However, prices for food, clothing and fuel continued to escalate. Harry was doing less and less at work but his expenses were increasing. His bonus income disappeared because home sales were limping along. Harry and Tina still had the most beautiful home they had ever owned and a nice boat in the garage. They were being more conservative about using the boat because of the high cost of fuel. Except for the worry that haunted their dreams, life was good. They would just have to work a little harder. Tina decided to go back to work. Few companies were hiring and she settled on a menial job as a receptionist just to make a few extra bucks. Something called recession was being talked about on the evening news.

In 2007, as all the teaser interest rates offered in the first five years of millions of subprime loans adjusted back to the current and much higher interest rate, borrowers began to default. New home lending shrank rather violently. New home sales stalled. The boss told Harry he could either take a pay cut or be laid off. These were tough times and everyone would have to sacrifice to keep the company alive. Harry's income was reduced. Tina took on some house cleaning jobs on the weekends. The prosperity that had trickled down through the whole economy during the building boom had magically disappeared. Everyone's business contracted. The contraction was not gentle.

Harry and Tina had been in their dream home for nearly 5 years. They only had a few months left before their mortgage would adjust to the current prime interest rate plus two points. They both knew there was no way they could stay afloat when the new, substantially higher mortgage payments, were required. They tried to refinance, but since their overall income was lower than before, they couldn't qualify for a new conventional loan, even though the payments would be less than the adjusted rate they would have to pay on their so-called subprime loan.

Harry and Tina decided to sell. When the realtor came by, they were distressed to discover that the value of their home had plummeted to roughly the amount of money they owed on it. All of the money they had worked so hard to save was gone. The equity they were basing their hopes and dreams on was gone. If they sold now, they would walk away with nothing. All they would accomplish would be to get out of debt. In the next year, the value of their home would drop to the point where they actually owed more on it than it was worth. This is what Jefferson meant by, ***"Then by deflation."***

Depriving the people of their property: Harry and Tina struggled along trying to practice positive thinking in the hope that they could turn their situation around. They networked and searched for better paying jobs, but none were to be found in the midst of a recession. They spent the balance of their savings supplementing their income while trying to save their home. It was not to be. Sales of homes in their price range had essentially stopped. They defaulted on their loan payments in the third month after the loan adjusted.

Three months later, the money masters, who were still rolling in cash from all of the profits made during the credit binge of the building boom years, foreclosed. Harry, Tina and the kids, who were wondering how they would go to college next year, had difficulty scraping up enough money for the first month's rent on a small house in a starter home neighborhood. Harry lost his construction company job and went to work at Home Depot where he could apply his knowledge of building materials. Harry and Tina, who had been homeowners for the last 10 years, now had no home of their own.

Harry, Tina and their children, along with millions of other Americans, had been deprived of their property and their life savings in the biggest robbery in the history of humanity.

The people who had caused the economy to expand so rapidly by pouring money created from nothing into it, had walked away with hundreds of billions of dollars in interest and loan origination fees paid on loans of money created from nothing. They also walked away with the hard earned life savings of millions of Americans. None of them went to jail because nobody really understood who was to blame. Wall Street hadn't really done anything recognized by the authorities as being illegal.

The same people, who had willfully inflated the economy and benefited from that inflation, had now legally foreclosed upon Harry and Tina. They were the new owners of Harry and Tina's dream home, which they would eventually sell again by loaning more money created from nothing to the next buyer who could qualify.

The foregoing story may not have happened to you, but you probably know someone to whom it did happen on a greater or lesser scale. Harry and Tina's story is only one example of how Jefferson's Nightmare is coming to pass through the creation of money as credit. Real estate is not the only vehicle through which the confiscation of both wealth and freedom occurs.

Harry and Tina had no intent to defraud anyone. They were simply trying to operate the version of the American Dream they had been taught. Their motivation was to do well for themselves and their family. They hadn't been working in the business world long enough to realize they were victims of a regularly occurring cycle. They became painfully aware that somehow they no longer enjoyed the same level of freedom to pursue their dreams that they had only a few years before. Something huge and impersonal called "the economy" was apparently at fault.

***They didn't really understand why
their freedom had been lost.***

CHAPTER TWO

The Global Freedom Crisis

I'd like to suggest we are on the cusp of changes so profound that in 2020, only four years from now, we will have trouble remembering who we were in 2016. There are now more than seven billion humans on Spaceship Earth putting a strain on all the natural resource systems critical for our survival. For the first time since the possibility of nuclear annihilation surfaced, we are looking at the potential for a significant self driven human extinction event occurring as a result of non-nuclear causes.

Such an event could be triggered by a breakdown in our financial system resulting in a failure of our distribution system to deliver the food and fuel required for the daily sustenance of a large number of people anywhere on Earth.

Ultimately such an event could be caused by our own collective unwillingness or inability to embrace what it will take to create a sustainable world culture based upon cooperation rather than competition, victory and the servitude of the losers. When the winners of the business competition cause extreme damage to both their customers and their competition, we are forced to ask—What about the losers? What happens to them? When the bulk of society is heavily damaged by the winners, for their own financial gratification, don't we have an inherent responsibility to re-evaluate our system? Don't we have an obligation to consider the greater good of society as a whole? Isn't that why we rebelled against the aristocracy in 1776?

We are starting to ask ourselves—does our existing monetary system still represent the best chance we have for the proliferation of the world population? More and more people are convinced that such a system no longer represents humanity's best hope for survival, much less proliferation. Our existing monetary system had its place in history but is rapidly becoming obsolete.

Over the years I have observed a growing awareness in my peers that something is systemically wrong with the way we've organized human affairs. Jefferson's vision of the future was based upon a population of sovereign citizens working together to create a prosperous free and self governing society. He knew from personal experience that the ideal of real freedom meant freedom from debt.

He understood that to be in debt meant having to pay today and tomorrow for goods or services that had already been consumed. Jefferson was painfully aware that to be in debt meant to lose your freedom. Those who willfully organize our financial system to maneuver us into debt are boldly attacking our god given right to real freedom.

Worldwide debt has grown exponentially in the last six decades. An acquaintance of mine pointed out that nobody is forcing humankind to sign the loan papers. That's not entirely true. The price of goods and services has risen dramatically in the last 20 years while incomes have actually lost ground.

"Total worldwide public and private credit market debt has risen from 40 trillion in 1994 to 200 trillion at present."
David Stockman

Despite what we've been told, massive inflation has increased the price of goods and services relative to earning power so much that almost no one is capable of buying a house, a car or any other major purchase with cash. The options have become, use debt to acquire what you want or go without. That is just one of the ways we have all been sucked into the current financial system. In 1776 we measured the U.S. national debt in millions. During the civil war our debt was measured in billions. Today it is measured in trillions of dollars. To give you a little perspective on the magnitude of a debt measured in trillions:

One million seconds = 11.57 days
One billion seconds = 31.70 years
One trillion seconds = 31,700 years

The growth of worldwide debt has been willfully created by an identifiable group of people as a method for covertly transferring both wealth and freedom from the average person to a very few at the top of our socio-economic structure. This is being accomplished through the processes of inflation, deflation and indebtedness. When you are in debt to someone, the freedom you enjoy to live life the way you want is diminished. The process of maneuvering people into debt is the essence of Jefferson's Nightmare.

The people who run the worldwide money printing scam, create and then detonate one financial bubble after another, taking the profits and leaving the losses to everyone else. There is a short period of calm while they shift from real estate to stocks or to war, then it's back to business as usual. It's as if we pushed all the weight to one side of the boat and are wondering why it's capsizing!

Most people I talk to are asking, "Where did the money go? We used to have money and then it disappeared. Where did it go? We used to have opportunity and then it disappeared. Where did our opportunity go?" We nod our heads sagely and summarize by saying, "Yes, these are difficult times, the economy is bad." Then we go on as before, working harder and harder to keep from going backwards. It's not obvious whom to call or what to do to change the circumstances that surround us. But, things are changing. As we investigate the causes of our collective misfortune the men and women behind the curtain are coming into view.

I'm not an economist, so the conclusions I've presented in this book are the result of a regular guy just trying to figure out what the hell actually happened during his lifetime. If you add up the national debt of all the countries in the world and try to analyze who owes what to whom, the numbers don't match. That is to say, debtor nations seem to have more debt than creditor nations claim they are owed. We constantly hear about the oppressive national debt of nearly every country. How can nearly every country in the world be in debt? Is there one giant mystery country that we all owe massive amounts of money to? No, there isn't. This level of debt exists because national and international debt is not just an affair between nations.

If you ask people on the street who the countries of the world owe their national debt to, the prevailing answer is, "The nations of the world owe their national debt to each other, don't they?" If America owes Japan and Japan owes America, then we should be able to begin zeroing out opposing debts reducing interest costs and making life simpler for everyone, right? Not exactly.

The current level of worldwide debt exists because countries are made up of corporations and corporations are made up of

the people who own them. In the final analysis all of our mas-
sive national debts are not owed by one country to another, but
by the population at large to a small group of individuals who
control the world's financial systems.

How did that happen on such an unprecedented scale? A recent computer study by theorists at the Swiss Federal Institute of
Technology in Zurich analyzed 37 million companies and investors revealing 1,318 complex interlocking ownerships that
control the majority of the world's large blue chip firms.[1] Further analysis distilled that number down to 147 "super entities"
that control over 40 percent of world wide wealth. Who are
these people? Why have they created such a heinous way of acquiring wealth? Do they care about the condition the world is
in? Do they care about you and how your life is playing out?

In previous books I referred to them as the Grey Men because
they seemed to operate in the shadows behind the dark veil of
doublespeak that masquerades as modern financial culture. A
dear friend kept referring to them as the Dominators. The more I
turned that over in my mind the more I felt the term "Dominator" was much more expressive of who they are. I have adopted
it and consider the terms to be synonymous. As I watched the
tragedy of the global financial crisis unfold from the front row,
my awareness of whom and what they are has changed. Early on
I thought of them as a small group of very powerful elitists.
Now, I understand that the elitists are indeed there, but again,
there is more to the story about how they rose to power and how
they stay in power.

How did such a small group of individuals acquire such a
large share of all wealth? Are they millions of times more productive than everyone else? Absolutely not. Are they so creative
and have improved the lives of the world population so much
that they deserve the lion's share of everything? Only a very few

have brought that level of light and innovation to the world. Bravo to the people who are improving the lives of everyone. They deserve our respect and admiration. However, we need to be very concerned about the Dominators who do not innovate but simply feed off of society.

Do they actually create wealth or have they slowly convinced all of us that the steady confiscation of the wealth of average citizens is a legitimate business activity?

Decades of thinking about who these people are lead me to the conclusion that what they have in common is a belief system. It's a belief system that extends from the top all the way down to many of your neighbors and friends. It's a belief system that has millions of understudies who are ready and willing to take their place in the hierarchy if they can just be lucky enough to get the chance. It's a belief system that worships material and assigns no value to the real meaning of freedom.

I have come to call this belief system "The Dominator Agenda," and the people who practice it, "The Dominators." This book is about who they are, what they believe, and more importantly, how much we have all become like them. If you haven't been exposed to a realistic description of how the world really works, you may find some parts of the subject matter to be a little depressing.

One of my friends refers to this body of information as, "The facts that make you want to drop out and move off the grid." Be that as it may, most of humanity seems to learn by hindsight. We don't seem to see really nasty events preparing to transpire until after they do. In order to perceive what is about to transpire, it is necessary to understand what has actually happened to our world over the last 60 years. If we understand where we've been, it will be easier to see where we might be going.

Like a ship of death, looming out of a stinking fog, something called The Global Financial Crisis emerged from the self serving gloom of Wall Street in 2008. Few people saw it coming. Harry and Tina's story is only one small part of the far reaching effects of money created as debt. The Global Financial Crisis was caused by the creation of money as debt. The carnage inflicted on small business by the crisis was spectacular. Nearly everyone knows someone who lost their business or their jobs in the last eight years.

The willfully created processes of inflation, deflation and re-possession created by the Dominators of the Aristocracy of Capital represent a direct attack on the freedom of common men and women everywhere. The global financial crisis instilled in me the deep suspicion that the entire world financial system is rigged from top to bottom. There is something very rotten about the way it's been set up.

Apparently the financial carnage isn't over just yet. Wall Street appears to have learned nothing about sustainability since the bursting of the real estate bubble in 2008. In 2016 they are inflating a stock market bubble to unprecedented levels by pouring money created as debt into stock purchases. In the very same way they blew hot air into the real estate bubble, the Dominators are now inflating the stock market using the same methodology.

Something called a price/earnings or PE ratio tells the tale. Very few people can buy whole companies the way an ordinary citizen would buy a house. The stock market exists to sell portions of companies or shares, as they are known, so an investor can own small pieces of different companies. Essentially, the price of a share multiplied by the total number of shares equals the price or value of the company. The price a company costs is reflected in its price/earnings ratio. Calculating the value of a company is a more complicated process than I'm about to describe. However, to illustrate a point, let's say a company has a

PE ratio of ten and earns a net profit of one hundred thousand dollars, that company is said to be worth ten times its net profit or one million dollars.

Over the last few decades PE ratios of 10 to 16 have been normal. When the real estate bubble blew, only a few people were able to qualify to borrow money created from nothing with which to buy real estate. Our central bankers needed another vehicle in order to keep inflating the money supply. Rather predictably, they decided to shift from pumping credit into real estate, to pumping credit into the stock market. In the very same way money created from nothing as credit inflated housing prices it is now inflating stock prices.

The evidence is lodged in price/earnings ratios of 20, 25 or even 30. Those PE ratios are a direct indication of a highly overvalued stock market. Remember, that is what happened right before the real estate bubble blew! House prices reached an all time high driven by the inflationary pressure of money created from nothing as debt. That is exactly the same thing that is happening right now in the stock market. Wall Street, our government and the Federal Reserve are all colluding to produce a stock bubble of massive proportions. They are planning to keep pumping hot air into this bubble until it pops.

Why? Because they are making enormous amounts of money by doing it and are not willing to look beyond their short term goals of accumulating wealth at everyone else's expense. Are they really so stupid they can't see what they are creating? No, they aren't that stupid. They are simply willing to sell everyone else down the river in a last ditch effort to make as much money as possible before the party is over.

Remember how the over production of money created from nothing as credit caused the real estate bubble to detonate? Remember how Harry and Tina were deprived of a portion of their freedom as a result? We went to war against the British Aristocracy to establish our independent freedom. We went to war against communism, fascism and dictatorship to preserve that freedom. At the same time we have been giving so many lives to defend the ideal of freedom that we so cherish, we have also allowed ourselves to be dominated from within. This is the nightmare that haunted Thomas Jefferson's dreams.

The spiritual foundation of the United States of America is under attack by people who subscribe to a selfish and non-regenerative belief system. They create and then detonate one financial bubble after another. They are leaving widespread economic destruction behind, as they celebrate their good fortune. Unfortunately these are the political and financial leaders of our country. These are the people we have traditionally held in high regard as the ones who should know how to keep our country strong and viable.

Our financial system has been adopted around the world. Every country that allows its private banks to control the issue of currency first by inflation and then by deflation is participating in the creation of a Global Freedom Crisis. The people who are in charge of the issue of currency do not stand for freedom for common people. The plantation owners of Jefferson's day did not want to give up the slaves that were the foundation of their great fortunes. Nor do the modern financiers of today want to give up the wage slaves that are the foundations of their great fortunes. Who are these people?

They are the Dominators.

CHAPTER THREE

Who Are The Dominators and What Do They Want?

The OXFAM Report[2]
January 21st, 2014 Reuters News Service:

According to OXFAM Briefing Paper 178:

"The richest 85 people on planet Earth now own more wealth than the bottom half (3.5 billion people) of the entire global population. This massive concentration of economic resources in the hands of a few people <u>represents a significant threat to inclusive political and economic systems.</u>

Instead of moving forward together, people are increasingly <u>separated</u> by economic and political power, inevitably heightening social tensions and increasing the risk of <u>societal breakdown.</u>"

The OXFAM report contains an additional shocking statistic:

"The wealth of the top one percent of the richest people in the world is equal to 65 times the wealth of the entire bottom half of the world's population."

Who Are The Dominators?

Domination Defined: The word "dominate" means to influence, control, or rule by superior power or authority, to occupy the pre-eminent position, to order or command imperiously. How did the world become so stratified with such a small group of the ultra wealthy at the top of societal structure? How did so few people acquire the ability to dominate so many others? We all know of people that occupy such positions of power in the world. When you inquire into who those people might be, you don't think of the simple hard working folks in your life like your plumber, grocer, or mechanic. You think of people who are in positions that allow them to manipulate large numbers of fellow humans against their collective will. These folks tend to be the dictators, corporate CEO's, politicians and central bankers we hear so much about.

For thousands of years we have been convinced that a system wherein a small percentage of the population controls everyone else is the natural order of human affairs. However, due to higher and higher levels of worldwide connectivity, humanity is comparing notes. Common people everywhere are asking why is the world this way? Does it have to be this way or do we have choices? We are gradually waking up to realize that the current system is about the economic enslavement of the many by the few. That is why the distribution of wealth is so uneven.

Somewhere in the not too distant past we determined that we could no longer put a happy face on physical slavery. As the technology of mass communication became commonplace we could no longer hide the pain and suffering of an entire race of people behind the seeming gentility of the lifestyle lived in the plantation's big house. We fought for and then celebrated the end of slavery in America. But enslavement didn't really end, it just changed form. While we were busy for the next hundred and fifty years trying to manifest equality of opportunity for all races, creeds and colors, the slave masters were busy reinventing an equal subjugation of all of us in a much more powerful and covert form: ***Debt.***

Without regard to race, creed or color and so gradually that we didn't really notice what was happening, common people everywhere have been turned into indebted wage slaves.

> ***A Wage Slave** is someone who must dedicate his or her future labor to pay for goods that have already been consumed or are already in their possession.*

The term "wage slave" implies that the wage earner does not make enough money to purchase outright what they need for a reasonable standard of living and must go into debt to obtain those things. Wages are then seen, not as equity with which to acquire the necessities of life, but as money used to service debt. In Parts I & II of this book we will visit, in layman's terms, how wage slavery has become the common plight of most global citizens.

> ***Those who don't have capital must borrow***
> ***from those who do in order to exist.***

How did that become our reality? This is the dynamic created by the Dominators, who currently run the worldwide financial system. What is a Dominator? For most people, being dominated by another human is not an intrinsically pleasant experience. When you enter into a relationship with a Dominator you don't get to do what you want to do. You experience a loss of freedom. When you sign the loan papers for the short-term material gratification you wish to possess, you are agreeing to dedicate a portion of your future time left on the planet to do what your creditor wants you to do—pay the bill with interest.

When you borrow to live, you are literally selling your future.

The condition of being dominated means that you have experienced a loss in your ability to express your own free will in favor of having to use your future physical labor to execute the will of another. One of the constituent parts of being dominated is a loss of freedom. One of the constituent parts of the solution is the idea that all humans should enjoy an unalienable right to freedom. The most attractive aspect of freedom is the ability to decide for yourself what you will do with the remaining time available to you on the planet, unrestricted by the desires of others.

Who Are The Dominators? When I first started looking into the concept of the Dominators I floated a few hypotheses to test my ideas. Early on I thought, "Dominators must be a class of people. All rich people (the ten percent at the top) must be Dominators." No sooner had I adopted that idea then I ran into one very nice wealthy person after another who expressed no intent to dominate me in any way. In fact, some of them expressed a deep interest in helping me achieve my own highest level of prosperity.

So that wasn't quite right. Then I thought, "It must be the reverse, not all rich people are Dominators, but all Dominators are rich people." That made sense for a while. Then, I discovered that there are tons and tons of people who want to dominate me and usurp my right to express my own free will who are not even close to being rich. That idea didn't pass the test either.

Then I mused, "It must be all about big business." Most everyone is aware of the activities of big corporations that are constantly creating unjust monopolies so they can control the market and set a confiscatory price for a particular commodity. Then, I discovered, even though they are a minority, there are some very responsible corporations whose managers consider giving a high level of value for every dollar received to be the highest business ethic.

That wasn't it either. I was wracking my brain trying to understand what is it that sets a Dominator apart from other humans? After banging my head on the wall for years it occurred to me that the Dominators aren't a particular class of people identified by what they have acquired in life, but a belief system. The Dominator Agenda is a belief system that can be summarized by the answer to one central question:

The Dominator Question:

Are you willing to take unfair physical or monetary advantage of other human beings for your own personal material gain?

If you answered yes to that question, then, by this definition and regardless of the economic station you presently occupy in life, you are a Dominator. Dominators exist in every culture, social stratum and economic class. In their most egregious form, they are bound together by their ability and willingness to sacrifice the future labor and in many cases the lives of fellow humans for their own personal material gain. The Dominator Agenda is effective whether the ruling party is left, center or right because it operates above and owns the political process. For the most part being dominated is no longer a death sentence in the same way that physical slavery was. At least not in the short term.

What it does mean is to be slowly and covertly bled and fed upon all the days of your life.

When you were young you probably agreed to this arrangement willingly in trade for a few shiny objects of your desire. When you are older and the thrill of acquiring one shiny new object after another has subsided, the eventual effect is:

Terminal fatigue and loss of longevity.

As we shall see, this paradigm is no longer sustainable and represents a serious threat to the future existence of humanity aboard Spaceship Earth.

What do the Dominators want? The answer to that question can be summed up in a single word—More. They want more. They want more money, more power, more possessions, more prestige and more control over others. That's what is driving the statistics quoted in the Oxfam Report. The reason worldwide wealth is distributed so unequally is because the Dominators have achieved a level of success at acquiring an unfair advantage over both their competition and their customers on a scale that is unprecedented in the annals of human history. The fact that I have used the words *unfair advantage* would seem to imply that there is some sort of morality at play here.

An Unfair Advantage: What is an unfair advantage? In this context we don't need to be too concerned about the baby Dominator who takes unfair advantage of you by not returning the lawn mower he borrowed. That problem is not out of your reach and can be solved locally.

We do need to be concerned about the mature Dominators, and the companies and political organizations they inhabit, which have the ability to take unfair advantage of hundreds of thousands, millions or even billions of common people in a way that offers them no recourse.

I'll define it this way—an *unfair advantage*, in this sense, is a *form of leverage* used to manipulate one's customers and one's competition that is available at a regional, national or global level only to the holders of large amounts of capital, and not available to those who have no capital.

Is it imperative that the holders of capital use such techniques to acquire a larger and larger share of all wealth that exists on the planet? No it is not. They do it because they want more. They do it because they believe that "more" is the natural objective of all successful humans and the path they must trod to get what they want.

Those who engage in this behavior want you to believe that domination is the natural order of things. They believe they are simply bigger, faster and smarter, or nastiest of all, that they are hereditarily superior to the people they manipulate. They believe they deserve everything they are capable of confiscating. Again, I don't want you to think that I am condemning all the holders of capital. I will make an effort not to do that.

There are a lot of good people out there who do have a sense of fairness in business and in life. It is the Dominators who freely employ the covert techniques of financial subjugation that we need to understand. The Dominators you should be concerned about are the ones who wield the power to change the circumstances of your life in a negative way, from afar, without your prior knowledge or permission. If your experience is like Harry and Tina's you know how unpleasant that can be.

A Moral Imperative: I believe there *is a moral issue* before us. I base that claim upon the idea that the freedom to enjoy life, liberty and the pursuit of happiness is the cosmic intent for all human beings. Jefferson believed we have a god given right to freedom. I too, see that freedom clearly as being a part of the actual design of the natural world. No being in the natural world is in debt. Debt is a manmade contraption.

I believe that the founders of our great nation were divinely inspired to realize the cosmic intent of freedom in the political system they were creating. Somehow, that inspiration has been subverted over the last 240 years. I hope to demonstrate that those who willfully rob another of even a portion of that freedom not only do great harm to other individuals, but a greater harm to the future of humanity as well. That idea is becoming more and more obvious to people who have not been seduced by the short term pleasures of the Dominator Agenda and who do not practice the domination of others.

As we go forward I'd like to be fair and equitable in outlining how we came to be where we are and what there is to do about it. Most books exploring this subject matter will lose the reader in percentages of gross domestic product, trade imbalances and the effects of derivatives trading. I'll try to keep that to a minimum. There is a reason that the financial world is so complicated. The people who run it don't want the average person to know what's really going on.

"It is well enough that the people of the nation do not understand our banking and monetary system, for if they did, I believe there would be a revolution before tomorrow morning." Henry Ford

I want to tell the story behind Mr. Ford's remark in such a way that you will understand why he said that. I'd like to tell this story in such a way that regular folks everywhere can understand what's been done and what is at stake for our future. There is a common characteristic that runs through the worldwide banking system. It lays the foundation for all the confiscatory financial devices the Dominators have used to gain the current level of control they enjoy. This common characteristic has seriously affected your life, though you may not be aware of it.

The Dominators have taken control of our systems of exchange in order to build the world we now live in according to a very ignorant, narrow and unsustainable belief system. They have been extraordinarily successful in making their world our world. In their mad rush to acquire money, sex, power and status they have created a system that literally harvests the lives of common people everywhere. The Dominators have created a world that places the material interests of the few above a mutual respect for the sanctity of human life.

Here's how they did it.

CHAPTER FOUR

Money For Nothin

Gold, silver and copper have been in circulation and used as a medium of exchange since early Egyptian times. Over the centuries, precious metals gained in popularity as a medium of exchange for two reasons. First, precious metals have intrinsic value in that they can be made into useful and beautiful objects. Secondly they vastly simplified certain financial transactions by eliminating the need to match up buyer and seller in a barter type situation.

Let's say you had several hundred chickens that you wanted to trade for a few horses. But the person who had the horses you so badly wanted wasn't interested in owning chickens. With precious metal money in circulation, you could go to a third party who did want chickens and exchange them for the appropriate amount of gold, silver or copper. You could then transport the much smaller volume of precious metal to the horse trader and purchase the horses you wanted. In this manner, precious metals simplified the flow of commerce and remained the preferred medium of exchange in the world at large for several thousand years. Paper money first came into use in China during the 7th century. The widespread use of paper as money did not take hold in Europe for another thousand years. Following is the generic story of how it happened.

<u>Somewhere in Europe during the 17th century:</u> The time honored trade of goldsmithing can trace its roots nearly to what is thought of as the dawn of human history. Then, as now, goldsmiths served the upper echelons of society by crafting beautiful golden artifacts to be worn by royalty, the clergy and the merchant class as a symbol of power. It was common for wealthy people to wear gold chains that could be used as money simply by cutting off a link or two in exchange for goods. The gold trade had become relatively sophisticated from the earliest times and the goldsmiths possessed the technology both to weigh gold and determine its purity. In addition to the tools required to craft gold, the goldsmiths also needed to have a vault to store it in and the muscle to protect the vault from thieves.

When a merchant accumulated a quantity of gold that exceeded his daily requirements for conducting business, he needed a safe place to store it. The obvious choice was to deposit his gold with the goldsmith who already possessed the facilities needed to ensure its safety. So the merchant would bring his gold to the goldsmith and rent space in his vault. The goldsmith would take the merchant's deposit, place it in a pile on a shelf in the vault and label it with the merchant's name. Then the goldsmith would make an entry in his ledger recording the transaction. The merchant could then come by the goldsmith's shop and verify that his gold and the gold of others was still in the vault in little piles with all their names clearly visible.

When the goldsmith took a deposit in this manner he also wrote the merchant a receipt that bore the merchant's name, the amount of gold on deposit and a promise to pay the merchant his gold upon demand, minus a small fee for storage and protection. When the merchant needed more money to make a purchase than he had in pocket change, it was still necessary to go to the goldsmith, make a physical withdrawal, take the gold to the site of the transaction, verify its weight and purity and do business. The process was cumbersome and it became clear in a very short period of time that the paper receipt issued by the goldsmith would be accepted in lieu of the physical gold by more and more people. It would be accepted because everyone knew they could go to the goldsmith and cash the receipt for real gold at any time.

By and by the merchants began to request that the goldsmith issue many receipts in smaller amounts than the total deposit held in the vault to make the exchange of receipts (paper promissory notes), for goods and services, more convenient for all. This the goldsmiths were very willing to do since it was clear they were beginning to make more money renting space in the vault than they were earning by actually making artifacts out of gold.

The more convenient they could make the use of their gold backed receipts, the more customers beat a path to their door to rent space in the vault. They were anxious to service the needs of this new form of clientele. They didn't stop being artisans, but they now understood that their businesses had two separate divisions. The receipts issued by the goldsmiths had become the first practical gold backed paper money, the goldsmiths themselves had become the first modern bankers.

Many of the goldsmiths belonged to trade associations known as guilds and would meet periodically with their colleagues from other towns and cities to discuss the secret aspects of their businesses. Merchants who were traveling were making requests to be able to deposit gold with their home town goldsmith, carry the paper receipts to another town and withdraw gold from a colleague known to their own goldsmith. Members of the goldsmith guilds realized they could charge another fee for this service and organized themselves to accommodate the merchants by adding this feature to the growing list of financial products they were offering.

As time went by it became apparent that the practice of segregating each depositor's gold into separate piles and labeling it with the depositor's name, as well as writing the depositor's name on his receipt, was no longer necessary or desirable. The merchant didn't care whether the physical gold he withdrew had been previously owned by him or not. All the merchant cared about was having access to the equivalent amount of gold he had on deposit in whatever town he happened to be in. In some ways it was desirable for the merchant's receipts not to bear his name since in that way the history of his transactions could not be traced.

The goldsmiths found that erasing the identities of the owners of the gold in their vaults was of advantage to them as well. Any depositor could come to the goldsmith's shop and still see the now single pile of gold in the vault which gave them great comfort. They could still withdraw their gold upon demand as before, it simply no longer had their name on it.

This seemed like a reasonable thing to do making the process more standardized for everyone. As the goldsmith's business increased, and the issuance of receipts became commonplace, the goldsmiths noticed something very interesting. Now that their gold receipts were anonymous, they could occasionally issue a bogus receipt for gold they had not received and it would be honored at face value by all of those people who had become used to accepting the receipts in lieu of gold!

Very quickly the goldsmiths realized that they could actually create money out of nothing by writing anonymous receipts for gold they did not possess. Did you get the full impact of the last sentence?

The goldsmiths discovered that they could make money out of nothing!

Nobody would ever be the wiser since they could all come and still see the pile of gold in the vault but had no way to compare the pile of gold to the total face value of all the receipts in circulation. This was a potentially dangerous situation because the goldsmith was issuing more promises to pay than there was gold in the vault. If a circumstance occurred, such as a war, when all the depositors got scared and wanted their gold back at the same time, the truth would come out—there was not as much gold in the vault as there were receipts to claim it. Thus there would be a run on the bank and the goldsmith would be ruined, imprisoned or killed.

To combat this problem the goldsmiths came up with an ingenious plan. Instead of writing bogus receipts to spend directly, they would write bogus receipts (banknotes) and loan them out to be repaid with interest by the borrower. They were still creating money out of nothing, but when the bogus money was paid back, in a sense it ceased to exist, having never been real in the first place. However, the interest being paid was real and the goldsmith, having become dependent on the interest for his main source of income, realized that to keep the interest flowing he would need to keep loaning out the bogus bank notes.

The goldsmiths learned that they could protect themselves by requiring that their borrowers put up collateral in the amount of the loan. Each bogus bank note loaned by the goldsmith in this manner represented a promise to pay by the borrower. If all the goldsmith's notes were presented for payment in gold at the same time, the goldsmith would not be able to pay in full, but could point to the borrowers and say they owed the missing balance. If the borrowers could not come up with the repayment, the goldsmith could repossess their collateral, sell it for gold, and be made whole. Very quickly the goldsmiths discovered that the business to be in was the business of loaning money. They began to gear up to loan more and more of their bogus bank notes (paper money).

The people of the kingdom had never borrowed money before. Very quickly they discovered that by borrowing money they could afford to buy goods that up until now had never been available to them. The merchants were beginning to show them that they could have and enjoy fine fabrics, spices, salt, sugar and even coffee from exotic lands. They could have the new family wagon they so desired or the horse to pull it.

They were in for some hard lessons. It didn't take long for them to discover that in many cases the debt they incurred outlasted the goods they acquired or consumed. Then they were faced with the prospect of having to buy more new goods to replace the goods that had already been consumed or worn out, while still paying for the original goods. That meant borrowing more money. But, the economy was good, everyone was doing well and they felt they would be able to make up the difference in the future.

The goldsmiths were deliriously happy with their newly discovered ability to literally **make money** out of nothing and expressed their good fortune by adopting opulent lifestyles. The average person didn't understand what the goldsmiths were actually doing. Everyone thought the goldsmith's prosperity was the result of them being good businessmen and were therefore encouraged to do business with them.

However, there was another problem to be solved. Each time the goldsmith made a loan he recorded the transaction in his ledger. Each loan was recorded as a liability against the total deposit of gold in the vault. Anyone who had the authority to inspect the goldsmith's books, such as the king's tax collector, would discover that the amount of liabilities recorded greatly exceeded the value of gold in the vault and the books did not balance.

The solution to this problem was as easy as kiss my hand. All the goldsmiths had to do was to record the loans they made as assets represented by promises to pay, instead of liabilities represented by the absence of gold in the vault. The borrowers had put up collateral in the amount of the loans to back up the claim that the loans were assets and not liabilities.

Low and behold, the books balanced again and everyone was happy. Now, the goldsmiths were free to loan as much bogus paper money as they could find clients to borrow it and the books would stay balanced. As the money lending business increased, the amount of gold in the vault represented a smaller and smaller fraction of the total amount of paper money in circulation. As we all know, the process of printing more and more money, backed by the same amount of redeemable value, leads to an overall loss in the value of the currency. This is what we refer to today as inflation.

Inflation is a hidden tax payable by all users of a currency that flows to the operators of the currency system.

That tax is automatically confiscated from all who possess the currency, without their knowledge or permission, as a loss of purchasing power. Then another problem arose. The king's tax collector, who always had trouble collecting all the taxes the king wanted, figured out the scam and told the king. The next day a file of soldiers arrived at the goldsmith's shop and escorted the goldsmith to an audience with the king. The tax collector had explained the goldsmith's business to the king in detail and instead of imprisoning the goldsmith, the king informed him that he now had a new business partner. Together they would create an entirely new way of doing business. This entire business model was fraud on a grand scale and both the goldsmith and the king knew it well, but it was so lucrative they couldn't stop themselves from printing their fake money.

After a time, the paper notes began to be so common and so easy to get (easy credit, sound familiar?) that the people began to lose confidence in them (consumer confidence). After a while they started to raise prices for their goods and services to compensate for the loss of purchasing power they were feeling in their lives. Higher prices caused the economy to slow down and the king's treasury suffered from lack of both tax and interest revenue.

Then the king had an inspiration. He told the goldsmith to acquire the brand new invention known as the printing press and to put the king's name and eventually his likeness on the bank notes. Voila! The whole business was no longer a scam, it had just become legal! (It was and is still a scam.)

The new paper money was accepted by the people with enthusiasm. After all, it bore the king's name instead of the goldsmith's and his direct promise to pay in gold. Since the king was known to be the largest holder of gold in the kingdom, the people were mollified, consumer confidence went up and prices went back down. More and more people came to the goldsmith shop, which had been relocated to a space next to the palace, requesting new loans.

The king's interest income was restored, business activity improved and tax revenues increased as well. Both the king and the goldsmith were rolling in real money paid to them as interest on loans of fake money created out of nothing. In the meantime the common people were mired in more and more debt.

The kingdom itself was becoming a nation of wage slaves who were borrowing from the future in order to exist in the present.

CHAPTER FIVE

The Secret Money System: Foundation of the Dominator Agenda

The goldsmith story is a simple illustration of a modern process that hides behind an amazingly sophisticated veil of technological deceit. The first thing you may have noticed is that the goldsmith and the king (who were both Dominators) created a secret and self-serving financial system based upon a lie. The lie was that all the paper money the goldsmith printed represented actual gold in the vault. Today the process outlined in the foregoing story is referred to as ***"Fractional Reserve Banking"*** and is not only legal in most countries, it is the common characteristic behind almost all versions of the current worldwide financial system.

To make matters worse, the precious metal that used to back our modern currency has now been removed from the system altogether. The real value of the paper money in circulation is zero. It's just a paper promise that is being reneged upon on a daily basis. Whether you are aware of it or not, your life has been severely affected by this system. It constitutes a fraud that has been perpetrated against humanity on a scale now unprecedented in the history of our species.

Fraud: Fractional Reserve Banking is a fraud because it creates money out of nothing in the form of debt and enslaves people to pay that debt and the interest on it. When your bank accepts a $1,000.00 deposit from you they are allowed to turn around and loan out $900.00 of it to a third party. The remaining $100.00 must be held in reserve by the bank to fund daily operations and anticipated withdrawals. That $100.00 represents a Fractional Reserve of 10 percent. (Fractional reserve rates vary with the times. During the bursting of the real estate bubble in 2008 fractional reserve rates had been allowed to go as low as 3 percent!) Your bank is also allowed to tell you that they still have your $1,000.00 on deposit. That's the same as issuing fraudulent receipts for gold and saying that all the gold, represented by paper promises to pay, is in the vault.

How can your money be in two places at once? The answer is, the bank has just created 900.00 out of thin air by loaning it out as debt, while claiming they still have it on deposit. Creating money out of thin air "inflates" the overall money supply causing the existing money in circulation to be worth progressively less and less over time. Most relatively educated people today are aware that expanding the money supply by printing unbacked paper money dilutes the value of all currency in circulation and creates inflation. Creating money out of nothing as *debt* does the same thing. Inflation is the reduction in real value of the currency.

What could be purchased for 1 dollar in Jefferson's day costs 25 dollars today. We seem happy to write it all off with, "Life was just simpler in those days." We think price inflation is normal and it has become so. Most people do not understand that inflation is actually an undeclared tax levied on and gradually collected from all users of a currency without their knowledge or permission. The benefits of that tax, for which you never receive an invoice, are enjoyed by the people who are in control of the money system. In effect, that tax is levied against you as a confiscation of real value from your net worth making it impossible for the population at large to live in a debt free condition.

Debt: The second thing you may have noticed in the goldsmith story is that fractional reserve money is created as debt. When money is created as debt, the money to pay the interest due on that debt has not been created but must come from the existing money supply. The more debt that is created, the larger percentage of the existing money supply must be dedicated to paying the interest due on that debt. (You may have noticed that interest payments on our national debt are consuming a larger and larger percentage of our country's overall budget. This is starting to be the case all over the world.) That makes more and more money unavailable for purchasing real goods and causes a systemic shortage of cash.

Because there is interest due on the money, which has been fraudulently created, there will always be more debt than there is money to repay it.

If the king and the goldsmith (the government and the Federal Reserve) are printing more and more money and the wealth that money is supposed to represent is not showing up in your pocket, where did it go? The Oxfam report together with the goldsmith story tells you where it went. It went into the pockets of the people who are in control of the systems of currency exchange. You pay the ultimate bill for this activity. We have been occupying a planet shrouded in a willfully created fog of *artificial scarcity* that is growing at an exponential rate.

Under this system there never will be enough to satisfy the needs of everyone and periodic shortages of cash and goods will keep occurring.

There must be continual economic growth to fuel the confiscation of real wealth demanded by the operators of the secret money system. When overall growth slows down or stops, it's like a giant game of musical chairs. The music stops, a new recession appears, and millions of people are left with massive debt acquired in better economic times but no opportunity to earn the money to pay it off in the middle of a new recession.

You are seeing this taking place around the world right now. What's different about the current recession is, this time it's global in scope. The Fractional Reserve Ponzi Scheme[3] which is being promoted by Wall Street and our own Federal Reserve *is* the underlying structural cause of the continuing worldwide financial crisis that began to manifest in 2007 & 2008 and of which we have not yet seen the last.

Force: The third thing you may have noticed in the goldsmith story is that the king was able to become a partner in the goldsmith's lucrative business because the king controlled the use of force. The king had the soldiers he needed to enforce his claim against the goldsmith. The goldsmith didn't have force at his disposal. The Dominators at the top of the worldwide financial system are the people, who control the people, who control the use of force. Just stop paying your mortgage and if you don't leave willingly, you will eventually discover that the local sheriff, who is armed, will arrive at your door to remove you from the place you used to call home.

The people behind the sheriff, who will demand your removal, are the people who have loaned you the money, created from nothing, that you borrowed to buy it. Stop paying your mortgages en masse and you will see that a bigger force than the sheriff's department comes into play. No matter how screwed up it may be, our financial system is the law of the land. There are consequences for not obeying the law, even when the law is no longer just. You may recall, our country was founded to fight such injustice.

A Nation of Debtors: The fourth thing you may have noticed in the goldsmith story is that the secret money system ultimately created a nation of debtors. The people of the kingdom had been living on the land for centuries. The sacred knowledge passed down from parent to child for generations was about what to do today, to ensure survival tomorrow. Each child was taught the skills required to stay warm and fed throughout the changing seasons of the year. Prior to the arrival of the secret money system in the kingdom, the people had balanced the expenditure of their labor with their daily needs. They were well aware that what they did today ensured their comfort tomorrow. It was a simple life in harmony with the natural world that surrounded them. But, the people also wanted more.

When the king and the goldsmith adopted their scheme of creating money from nothing and loaning it out, they were literally confiscating real wealth from the people. But the people had balanced their labor with their needs and didn't possess great stores of wealth for the king and the goldsmith to confiscate. The king and the goldsmith had advertised to the people that they could have what they wanted *now* if they were willing to pay for it *later*. This development appeared to be a great innovation and held the promise of a higher standard of living for all. But where was this promised wealth to come from?

It was to come from the future!

The people were used to saving what they needed for tomorrow from the labor they produced today. As they became borrowers, they agreed to accept what they needed today and pay for it with the labor they would produce tomorrow, and the day after that, and the day after that. The common people were actually betting their freedom on their ability to continue to earn a living. If something happened to kill their crops or disrupt their jobs and they could not pay, they would be sentenced to debtor's prison to languish there until friends or relatives could extinguish their debt.

The modern equivalent of debtor's prison is a low credit rating that excommunicates you from the system of borrowing to satisfy your desires and implies that you have lost something of great value. If your only option to obtain the things you want in life is to borrow, then perhaps you have lost something of great value. The question that needs to be asked is:

Why is borrowing your only option?

In exchange for a few baubles today the people had mortgaged their most precious asset, their future. In a very real sense, the king and the goldsmith, owners of the secret money system, stole a portion of the people's labor from them at no cost, turned around and loaned it back to them at full value plus interest. The repayment of that debt by the people represented the loss of their future freedom.

That, my friends, is **SLAVERY**, made far more insidious because the enslaved do not understand what has been done to them. Your life has been seriously affected by the easy credit flowing from the seemingly innocuous institution of Fractional Reserve Banking.

"The few who can understand this system will either be so interested in its profits, or so dependent upon its favors, that there will be no opposition from that class, while on the other hand, that great body of people, mentally incapable of comprehending the tremendous advantage that <u>capital</u> derives from the system, will bear its burden without complaint and perhaps without even suspecting that the system is inimical to their interests."
Baron Mayer Amschel Rothschild. c1805

The Baron was right to declare that the great body of people have been bearing the burden of this system without even suspecting that something is not quite right. In his day, he may have been correct that they were mentally incapable of comprehending the system, but that is no longer true. Humans are much more educated than ever before. However, the Baron's secret money system remains hidden, though it still operates in plain sight.

When I started to do the research for this book, I interviewed a number of banking sector employees. What I found was shocking. The majority of people working in the banking industry as tellers, receptionists, new account executives and vice presidents of customer service, do not even recognize the term "Fractional Reserve Banking." These are regular folks doing compartmentalized jobs that are actually serving the Dominator Agenda without the slightest understanding of how the system really works. They are not Dominators themselves, but your friends and neighbors working in a service industry that claims its purpose is to help you manage your money.

That's why it's called the Secret Money System. It operates in plain sight, but even the people who manage its day-to-day affairs don't know how it really works.

However, if exposed to the truth, the great majority of everyday people in this country are now capable of understanding how the system works.

CHAPTER SIX

A Run on the Bank

The fraudulent game of Fractional Reserve Banking exists to take in deposits, lend them out and claim they are still in the possession of the bank. Why do banks fail? The most common cause of bank failures is non-performing loans. A handful of non-performing loans don't usually threaten a bank. As in any business, there are a certain percentage of transactions that fail. The bank has included a margin for loan failures in its business plan.

Local bank failures can certainly be caused by poor management. However, the bulk of bank failures occur when there is a serious downturn in the economy, people start losing their jobs, and then default on millions of loans that were once considered to be highly secure. That is what happened in 2007 & 2008. If the word gets out on the street that a bank may be going under, its customers might want their money back. The nightmare of all bankers comes on the day when all of the bank's customers arrive at once clamoring to withdraw their money. This is a calamity because despite the bank's claims, the customer's money isn't really there. The bank's promise to its customers is that they can withdraw their money on demand, but the bank has loaned out their money and cannot reclaim it on demand. Do you see the built in contradiction?

A run on the bank usually only happens in times of trouble like war, extreme civil strife or economic collapse. All of these events are times when you might actually want to have all your money, in cash, tucked away in your mattress. If all of the bank's customers show up demanding cash, the bank, not actually having your money in its possession, has no other option but to temporarily close its doors and appeal to the government for help. This is happening in Greece as I write these words. Part of the Greek solution is to close the bank's doors and allow its customers to withdraw only 60 Euros per day through the bank's ATM. They literally cannot get their money back.

The fact that no bank can survive the arrival of all of its depositors, asking for their money back on any given day, should tell you that our banking system is built upon a lie and is a house of cards.

Our government, knowing full well the fraudulent nature of Fractional Reserve Banking, created the Federal Deposit Insurance Corporation to insure your bank deposits up to 250,000 dollars and promote the idea that the system is solid. Each member bank pays the FDIC an insurance fee to cover the possibility of failure. If your bank over-leverages itself and fails, the FDIC will step in and, after a reasonable delay to allow for the necessary paperwork, will refund your money up to 250,000 dollars.

The FDIC proudly states that it is backed by the United States Government. What that really means is that during a systemic crisis like the financial crash of 2008 when hundreds of banks failed, the government of the United States covers the shortfall by printing the money to pay the bill. Well, they don't even actually do that. They just make an entry on a spread sheet. It doesn't really matter, the effect is the same. Creating money out of nothing, no matter how it is done, is the same as borrowing from the future. The problem is, it's your future. You and probably your children will be paying the bill for it.

So, here we have a financial system in which a very small group of people are allowed to create money from nothing as debt and charge massive amounts of interest for it. For the most part that group is allowed to walk away with the profits from this nefarious activity. When portions of that business scheme collapse you end up paying the bill...a second time, but in a way that prevents you from tracking where the problem came from. Nice huh?

The First Item in the Dominator Agenda is: *Gain control over a country's currency and establish Fractional Reserve Banking as the law of the land.*

<u>Money is Energy:</u> The money you earn represents your labor. The operators of the secret money system are literally feeding off of your future labor like so many vampires. That's right, the Dominators feed upon you like so many vampires! In the United States, modern money is no longer backed by precious metal but only by what is known as the full faith and credit of the United States Government.

However, the United States Government does nothing to actually earn money or create real wealth. The only revenues enjoyed by the U.S. Government come from taxes paid by individuals and businesses that actually do produce something and create real wealth. So, in effect the money printed by the U.S. Government, which is not backed by precious metal and having no real value of its own, is backed by the American people and represents their collective labor.

When the government and the financial sector squanders the money they confiscate from you, they are actually squandering your future labor. You notice this in your life when it costs more and more to buy a bag of groceries. You notice this in your life when you realize that you have to work harder and expend more energy to stay in the same place as before. No one fails to notice the terrifying feeling and mental strain of trying to keep from going under altogether. This terminal fatigue is now being felt by large numbers of baby boomers who have worked for forty years and are now watching their retirements literally being siphoned off by various Dominator devices.

How did we come to the place where nearly every household and every country in the world are heavily in debt?

CHAPTER SEVEN

The Tsunami of Debt

In the early part of the 20th century it was common for citizens to have credit accounts at individual stores. A credit card that could be used at more than one store wasn't available until 1950. Frank McNamara envisioned a card that could be used by traveling salesmen, who ate out frequently, while on the road. The Diners Club Card he invented would allow the traveling salesman to dine out every night and pay one bill at the end of each month. The salesman would also receive a statement showing all the places he dined and the cost for each meal, which information would be useful in filing his tax return.

In 1950, Mr. McNamara introduced his card to 200 friends and colleagues. By the end of that year he had 20,000 subscribers. It would be another 8 years before American Express and Bank Americard (Visa) entered the marketplace in 1958.

I was 9 years old when my dad obtained his first credit card. I remember my street was paved in red brick laid in a herringbone pattern, we had a party line telephone, milk was delivered by the milkman, our TV had a 12" screen housed in a wood cabinet, one of my heroes was Fess Parker, playing Davy Crockett, and we enjoyed watching the Little Rascals every Saturday morning.

My dad made around $11,000.00 in 1958, almost three times the national average for that year. We were considered to be well off. We laugh when we think of how low prices were in those days. I still remember the nickel candy bars that gave us such delight. Dad went to work and Mom stayed home to manage five kids. Nobody ever thought about day care or even the possibility that in the not too distant future both parents would have to work to stay afloat. Such a thing was beyond comprehension. It was normal for the full time labor of one man to support the needs of himself, his spouse, five children and even a grandparent or two.

If one man could support the needs of such a large family then and today it takes two adults working full time to support a family of four, what has changed? Has the amount of work a human being can do changed over time? Well, yes it has. It has increased. Modern technology makes it possible for one person to do much more work than they could in the 1950's. That means we should be able to work less and enjoy the same or a better standard of living? Right? Why is that not the case?

During my lifetime, our collective viewpoint of the money we earn to make a living has changed dramatically. Household income used to be considered something with which to buy goods directly, meaning that you enjoyed equity in what you owned. With the advent of the credit card, the American public began to carry more and more debt. Being able to buy whatever one wanted within one's credit limit was, for the first time, an integral part of the American Dream.

My grandparents, having been mature adults in business during the great depression of the 1930's, remembered the awful carnage inflicted on those who owed money and couldn't pay. Their direct experience in life caused them to be morally opposed to this new fangled idea of being able to incur more and more debt at will, just by signing your name. Despite the objections of the older generation, the trend toward more and more debt began to establish itself around the world. As this gradual change occurred in our attitude toward debt, something very strange happened. The confiscation of real wealth by the Dominators shifted into a higher gear. In retrospect, my first lesson on inflation hit me right where any kid would notice it. For as long as I could remember a Mars bar cost 5 cents. Suddenly, almost overnight, a Mars bar cost 25 cents and shrunk in size at the same time! I was crushed! I now had to do more chores than ever before to afford the same level of sugar saturation I had become used to.

I was, of course, unaware that the same process was also occurring in my father's life in much more critical ways. I wasn't aware that it had something to do with debt. If my father spent his entire 1958 salary of $11,000.00 directly on food, shelter, clothing and the normal everyday expenses of life, he could command $11,000.00 in goods and services. But, if he were approved to use his whole $11,000.00 salary just to service debt, he could command roughly 10 times that much or $110,000.00 in goods and services. (Then as now, lenders used a debt to income ratio for how much exposure they were willing to risk on any one individual.) Nevertheless, the giant gap between what could be enjoyed by paying cash and what could be enjoyed by incurring debt was gradually causing prices to inflate across all economic sectors.

An enormous vacuum between prices in an equity driven economy versus what prices could rise to in a debt service economy changed the structure of the American financial system. All suppliers of raw materials, all manufacturers and sellers of goods found they could raise prices at a higher rate than was demanded simply by the fractional reserve banking model. Prices began to surge during the 1950's and we called it "the magic of the American Dream." A Chevrolet Impala that cost $1,700.00 in 1958 goes for $27,000.00 in 2015. That is a real price increase of 1,588 % in 57 years. We have been convinced that rate of inflation is normal. Incomes began to increase as well but always at a slower rate than inflation. In 1975 a $100,000.00 salary was only enjoyed by CEO's of big corporations. Today a $100,000.00 salary is barely enough for a family of four with two kids on their way to college.

We tend to laugh at our nostalgia for the old prices. They were so quaint compared to today. Back then we just didn't know what life was going to be like in 2016. Today, household income is not measured as money to buy goods and services directly. Today, we measure success by how much debt one can service and what goods can be bought with that debt. Part of the problem is that if you owe a balance on goods acquired with debt, you don't really own them. You are just renting. Stop paying the bill and you will know what I mean.

Over the last sixty years, that seemingly subtle shift in orientation has been accompanied by massive inflation not only in the price of goods but in the amount of taxes, insurance and interest we all pay for those goods. The shift from equity to debt is a worldwide phenomenon. It would be highly naive to think that shift wasn't intentional.

The Second Item in the Dominator Agenda is: *Pump fake money into the worldwide financial system by encouraging household debt in the countries in which we have control of the currency.*

The purpose for encouraging household debt is to get billions of people paying back personal debt with interest that cost the Dominators next to nothing to create in the first place.

The Third Item in the Dominator Agenda is: *Pump fake money into the worldwide financial system by encouraging governments to overspend and take on debt.*

The purpose for encouraging governmental debt is to get billions of people paying back national debt with interest that cost the Dominators next to nothing to create in the first place. Out of 190 countries on the planet, there are only five that have almost no national debt—they are Brunei, Liechtenstein, Palau, British Virgin Islands and Macau.[4] Not exactly serious contenders for the title of the largest economies on the planet.

As of this writing, the national debt of the United States is just over 18 trillion dollars. That's $56,936 dollars for every man, woman and child in the U.S. population. That number adds up to a whopping $227,744.00 for every family of four people. That is the official number. If you add in the unfunded liabilities the United States Government is obligated to pay, the real number is much, much higher. You have not received an invoice for this amount, nor will you, but mark my words, you are paying the bill every month, and your descendants will continue to pay the bill long into the future unless some sort of mega-change takes place.

By mega-change, I mean a fundamental change in the way our financial system works.

The greatest scam in the history of money is the idea that anyone should be allowed to charge any kind of interest (much less compound interest) on money created from nothing. The very idea that this arrangement is normal or is a natural economic law is a deceit of the highest order. It serves only to convey special privileges upon the small segment of society that possesses large amounts of capital and in fact, is only one of the techniques they have used to become the holders of large amounts of capital.

Since the hidden costs of our monetary system are borne by the public, money should be a public utility.

Most economists agree that we must have an elastic money supply. They will tell you that the modern economic world operates at such a high rate of speed, that the money supply must be able to expand and contract along with the ebb and flow of commerce. They believe that a static money supply based upon precious metal would restrict commerce and inhibit economic growth rates around the world. I think that view is correct, up to a point.

Someone benefits from the elasticity of the money supply. Someone pays the bill for the elasticity of the money supply. Under our current system they are not the same people. No one should have the right to extract all the benefits of an elastic money supply for themselves and hold everyone else hostage for the costs. If we can't find a way to make that illegal, then we should find a way to return the benefits of the elastic money supply to the people who ultimately pay the bill; we the people.

We need to begin to look at our money supply as a public utility that exists for the common good. We need to restrict the ability of private banks to create money out of nothing as debt by demanding a much higher fractional reserve be kept in place than the current rate of 10 percent.

We need to remove The Federal Reserve from power and create a public utility board to oversee economic policy. That board must be fully insulated from all political and financial market influence. That board should be comprised of citizens that have been carefully selected according to a pre-determined criteria, to represent a fair cross section of every economic class.

Every member of that board should be prohibited from benefiting economically from any decision made by it. We need to return to honest monetary policy run by the people for the people, not by Wall Street on its own account.

The stated objective of the public utility of currency should be to reduce the overall debt of as many citizens as possible. The overall debt of the citizenry can be reduced by eliminating the ability of private parties to benefit from manipulation of the money supply. The overall debt of the citizenry can be reduced by putting the public utility board in charge of the interest rates that can be charged by anyone.

The public utility board would decide when and by how much it is appropriate to expand the money supply, not for the benefit of a few but for the benefit of society as a whole. If you were able to own your home in 10 years by paying its actual price, instead of five times its actual price, you would have much more disposable income to apply to other purchases. Your life would be different. The economy would be more vibrant. A strong middle class that owns its assets free and clear can only be good for the country.

As it is now, the tsunami of worldwide debt has carefully been engineered by the Dominators to place nearly everyone in the developed world into debt. The tsunami of worldwide debt is starting to curl at the top as it approaches the beach. When it finally hits the beach, the resulting carnage will be unprecedented in recorded history.

"It is said that the world is in a state of bankruptcy, that the world owes the world more than the world can pay."
Ralph Waldo Emerson

We are going to create a new world. The question of concern is—Will it be controlled by the people for the people according to the vision of our founding fathers? Or will it be controlled by the Dominators on their own behalf?

Who are the Dominators?

They are the people who have set up the systems that drain a significant percentage of your labor into their own pockets in return for nothing of real value. If we are to graduate from this system it will be necessary for a majority of us to understand how it works. Then we will need to bring hope, creativity and inspiration to the table to boldly make the changes that will form the foundation of a new world for all.

Never before, have so many owed so much to so few
in return for so little.

PART II

The Dominator Playbook

CHAPTER EIGHT

Breathe In Breathe Out

The Dominators have concocted a playbook of devices they have used very successfully to cocoon working people all over the world so they can be fed upon continuously.

The Dominators we should be concerned about are the ones who wield the power to change the circumstances of the lives of millions of people in a negative way without their prior knowledge or permission.

The next few chapters will describe some of the various techniques in the Dominator Playbook. There are thousands of variations on the ways that Dominators practice confiscating your labor. We couldn't possibly talk about them all, so we'll explore the most iconic versions to help you get the gist of what has been done and why the world is the way it is. Yep, this is the part of the information that makes you want to drop out and head for the hills, but bear up my friends. There are solutions. Once we understand what really runs the world, then we'll be able to have a meaningful discussion about what to do next.

Printed on your money are the words, "United States of America, Federal Reserve Note." Those words quite clearly imply that the money you use is issued and controlled by the government of the United States for the benefit of its citizens. It is true that our currency is printed by the United States Mint. However, the organization that issues and controls it is a privately held corporation. That's right, The Federal Reserve is not a federal institution, owned and operated by the government, in trust for the American people. Like the goldsmith's business, the Federal Reserve is a privately held corporation. The Federal Reserve does not put money directly in the pockets of the Dominators. That would be too obvious. However, Fed policy indirectly puts money in the pockets of the Dominators when it is used as the economic throttle (gas pedal) to regulate the speed of the economy of the United States.

Taken directly from the Federal Reserve website, the stated mission of the Federal Reserve is:

The Federal Reserve System is the central bank of the United States. It was founded by Congress in 1913 to provide the nation with a safer, more flexible, and more stable monetary and financial system. Over the years its role in banking and the economy has expanded.

Today, the Federal Reserve's duties fall into four general areas:

1. Conducting the nation's monetary policy by influencing the monetary and credit conditions in the economy in pursuit of maximum employment, stable prices and moderate long term interest rates.

2. Supervising and regulating banking institutions to ensure the safety and soundness of the nation's banking and financial system and to protect the credit rights of consumers.

3. Maintaining the stability of the financial system and containing systemic risk that may arise in financial markets.

***4. Providing financial services to depository institutions, the U.S.
government, and foreign official institutions, including playing a
major role in operating the nation's payment system.***

If you have been keeping up with the financial news since
2008 you can't help but ask if they seriously think the foregoing
is still believable? It is abundantly clear, to anyone paying attention, that we do not have a safer, more flexible and more stable
monetary and financial system since 2008. We do not have maximum employment or stable prices. The systemic risk that has
arisen in financial markets (Wall Street) has not been contained
and is now causing red lights to flash on financial dashboards all
over the world.

Using zero interest rate central bank money created from
nothing, Wall Street has caused stock prices to rise to price vs.
earnings ratios, so high they are absolutely ludicrous, and clearly
unsustainable. Be that as it may, I'm going to avoid a detailed
discussion of all the intricacies of the Federal Reserve itself.
There are plenty of good books that cover the subject in more
detail than I have room for here.[5]

I want to focus on describing the inflationary and deflationary economic cycles created by the Fed and Wall Street as a part
of the Dominator Agenda. I am going to be accused of massive
oversimplification for the following explanation. I'm content
with that because I want you to understand how the flow of energy that we think of as the "economy" is being manipulated by
the Dominators on their own behalf. While the details are so
complex they cause migraines in the heads of the most sophisticated economists, what we are really talking about is the rate at
which your personal labor is being confiscated from you. It is
truly that simple.

The Federal Reserve has control over what we will call (for our purposes) *"the federal funds target rate or the Fed rate."* Again the reality is intentionally complex, but for the sake of illustration let's say that the federal funds target rate is the rate you hear about in the news when it reports that the feds have raised or lowered the interest rate. Historically, when this interest rate went up credit requirements tightened, partly because a higher interest rate means one would have to qualify to pay a higher payment on any given loan. When credit requirements tighten, the economy slows down.

When this interest rate went down, credit requirements loosened and the economy sped up. Let's think of credit requirements as your personal debt to income ratio and payment history (credit score) plus the percentage of a down payment you would be required to have to buy a house or a car. When credit is loosened, typically down payments are reduced and it is easier to borrow and buy things. Under these artificially imposed conditions, consumer confidence is high and borrowers can scarcely be serviced fast enough.

Today, we find ourselves in uncharted territory. Interest rates are low, but consumer credit is being restricted by banks who don't want to lend in a risky economy. At the same time, stock market speculators are engaging in an unprecedented feeding frenzy fueled by a near zero central bank interest rate and loose commercial credit. The prolonged use of zero interest rate commercial credit means that the central bank can no longer reduce the interest rate to encourage economic growth. In a sense, the controls are broken. We've turned on the garden hose full blast and the end is gyrating about wildly. Today, the interbank interest rate is near zero and economic growth isn't happening. This configuration has never occurred before in the history of the Fed or of our country.

Historically, the Fed rate has acted as an economic gas pedal. Press the go pedal, the interest rate goes down, credit requirements loosen up, lending increases and economic activity expands. When the go pedal is pressed (by the Dominators) businesses crank up, the unemployment rate goes down, money is easier to come by and people spend more freely. They also acquire more debt in the process of spending more freely and inflation increases. I have outlined how the real estate bubble, which burst in 2008, was a product of easy credit and high inflation.

"Like gold, U.S. dollars have value only to the extent that they are strictly limited in supply. But, the U.S. Government has a technology, called a printing press, (or today, its electronic equivalent) that allows it to produce as many U.S. dollars as it wishes at essentially no cost. By increasing the number of U.S. dollars in circulation, or even by credibly threatening to do so, the U.S. Government can also reduce the value of a dollar in terms of goods and services, which is equivalent to raising the price of those goods and services. We conclude that, under a paper money system, a determined government can always generate higher spending and hence positive inflation."

Ben Bernanke Chairman of the Federal Reserve
November 2002

Why is positive inflation motivating to the Dominators? It is motivating because they make money from it. The Dominators own the rights to the raw materials used to make everything. They own the industries that make the big machines that are used to mine the raw materials that are used to make everything. They own the supply chains that support the companies that produce the rubber, steel, and glass used to make cars, machinery and appliances. They own the ships and railroads that are used to transport the raw materials and finished goods back and forth from the mines to the mills to the manufacturers to the assembly plants to the point of sale where you borrow the money to buy them.

They own the banks and finance companies that borrow the money the Fed created from nothing in order to mark up the interest and loan it to you to buy the goods they have manufactured. They own the finance companies that lend you the money to buy all of it. When borrowing increases during an inflationary cycle, all the sales figures of all of these activities increase.

The Dominators make fabulous amounts of money during the inflationary cycle (In Breath.) That's why they love inflation. They also provide many of us with jobs so we can afford to borrow money from them and assume the debt service on it. The curious thing about this arrangement is that, except for a very small percentage of the population, the jobs they provide don't pay enough for you to be able to buy the major things you want outright. So, you must borrow and participate in the secret money system to obtain what you want.

Welcome to the company store!

When the economic go pedal is pressed, the Dominators, who tend to have large stakes in the banks and credit card companies that benefit from increased economic activity, make money every time there is a transaction where money changes hands. They make money on the goods that were sold, they make money on the service fees associated with those transactions and they make money on the interest charged on the debt you assume. We are talking about trillions of dollars in transactions every week. Accomplished Dominators occupy the top slot in the economic food chain. They make massive amounts of money on all the interest that is being charged for all the borrowing that has been encouraged by their offering of cheap and available credit (in the form of money that has been created out of nothing.)

We know from the goldsmith story that the owner's of the secret money system can't pump fake money into the system forever. The reason is, printing fake money and pumping it into the money supply gradually decreases the value of all existing money. The system has a natural cycle.

If the currency loses too much value too quickly, the people who rely on it become fatigued and consumer confidence suffers as another inflationary cycle reaches its peak.

When consumer confidence suffers there is a corresponding drop in retail sales of all kinds. That's why the government tells you unemployment is only at 5% when 23% is closer to reality. That's why the government tells you that 300,000 jobs were created in December of 2015 when their number is just creative accounting. If consumers lose confidence, then the Dominators become concerned. It is better for them if the devaluation of the currency is so gradual it appears to be normal and the population at large doesn't notice. That way they can keep the charade going as long as possible. This phenomenon of economic expansion and contraction is referred to as "The Business Cycle."

The bill for the business cycle is paid by all users of the currency in the form of a loss in purchasing power. During my lifetime this cycle has peaked every 8 to 10 years. When the go pedal is pressed everything expands until it's about to burst. Lending is at an all time high, property values become ludicrous. Speculation is rampant. The last time we went through the end of that cycle was in 2007, right before the real estate bubble blew. This is what I mean by making money on the In Breath (the inflationary cycle.)

The Out Breath is a different story. Historically, when the Fed (which is owned by the Dominators) determines that the Dominator feeding frenzy has peaked on the up side and the currency cannot stand any more short term inflation without collapsing, it raises the Fed rate. Banks, credit unions and finance companies follow suit. Credit tightens up, borrowing is reduced, buying is reduced and the economy contracts. Rarely is that contraction gentle. It seems we all have short memories. In the anticipation of a continuing "good economy" thousands of companies have hired more people and borrowed more money than they are now able to service the debt on in the current economic downturn. When the economy starts to slow down, the difficulties begin.

A good example of what happens in an economic downturn is taking place where I live. Right after the crash of 2008 north west Montana was suffering for jobs. Quite a few people that I knew bought travel trailers and went to North Dakota to get jobs in the oil fields. With oil selling at over 100 dollars a barrel, the extraction of oil from the Bakken oil formation had finally become economically feasible. Many boom towns sprang up on the border between Montana and North Dakota to handle the influx of workers streaming in. American oil production increased rapidly and prices at the pump went down.

America was finally going to be well on its way to oil independence. Large numbers of companies financed oil drilling activities in the Bakken area with borrowed money, providing lucrative jobs to people that really needed somewhere to work. We all thought this would be a long term oil boom. Energy independence would be good for America.

The Dominators in a certain sandy country decided they had enough of the new competition. They pumped substantially more oil than usual intentionally creating a glut and driving the price of oil down to half of what it was. This is known as the free market, but in reality is a subtle form of war. At that price point, extracting oil from the Bakken formation was no longer economically viable for companies that had financed their growth with debt. Oil exploration companies that had borrowed too much money from the Dominators to drill and pump oil could no longer afford to keep paying both the principle and interest on their debt, and their rigs began to shut down one by one.

My friends and neighbors are now coming home to a valley which still hasn't recovered from the crash of 2008. There are no jobs for these folks, the value of their homes is less than what they owe and For Sale signs are popping up all around us. No sooner had the carnage put many of OPEC's competitors out of business, then gas prices, which had bottomed at 1.99 per gallon, started to increase once again.

Over the next year gas prices rose back to the 3.00 mark, as many small oil companies went under. OPEC thought they had sent the message they intended. But two things happened that they failed to foresee. First, the damage they inflicted on the American oil industry, was not as extensive as they thought it would be. Secondly, in order to save money in a tight job market, the public decided to cut back on driving. All of a sudden there was an unintended glut of oil on the market and gas prices started to go back down again.

Just the free market working its magic folks. Just the free market playing havoc with your life. These decisions have been made thousands of miles away by Dominators that neither know who you are nor care what happens to you.

Historically, homeowners have found themselves in a similar spot at the end of every inflationary cycle. They have borrowed more money to buy a nicer home or improve the home they own and are unable to service the debt on their new loans having lost their jobs or had their paycheck cut back. During the deflationary cycle production of all goods and services starts to ramp down and the bloodletting begins.

Our news programs (which are owned by the Dominators) tell us, "Darn the luck, the economy has turned down again, we will have to appeal to our politicians for a solution." Then our dummy politicians use the Dominator owned media to make a big show out of blaming the other side of the aisle for fiscal mismanagement. We all pick sides and the resulting brouhaha commands the news cycle. Nobody looks behind the curtain.

Nobody questions the very foundation of our system.

The next phase of the drama comes as the Dominators who have made the loans on all the business equipment and real estate bought during the In Breath begin to repossess the homes and assets of the small business owners that over extended themselves. This process is considered to be fair and equitable. You did, after all, default on your loan.

However, nobody seems to be pointing out that the Dominators were the ones who created the conditions under which you lost your job which is the reason you defaulted on your loan!

Remember that a condition of the loan you took out required you to put a percentage of money down on your purchase? That money, which in many cases, represents the life savings of the home or small business owner, who is being foreclosed upon, now belongs to the company that extended bogus credit to them in the first place. If you can't pay, you lose your investment.

Life looked so rosy when you took out the loan. You were upbeat and positive about the business you were in. As you sit and watch the mysterious forces of the economy wreak havoc in your life, there is no effective recourse for you. You can join the chorus, screaming at the politicians, who all promise to do better, if only they can stay in office, so they can fight the good fight against the other side of the aisle. It is the other side of the aisle, we are assured, who are the ones responsible for the current malaise. We re-elect our favorite legislators, but nothing changes. You executed your civic duty by voting. Beyond that there is no one to contact to alleviate your financial suffering. There is certainly nothing obvious to do except to work harder to keep from going backwards.

If you have been through this cycle you may have wondered—the real estate and businesses the Dominators are repossessing are no longer worth what they were at the peak of the cycle so what real advantage is there for the lender to foreclose? The answer lies in something the Dominators have that you don't.

They have the power to wait it out.

Because they have much more capital than they need to live, they can wait to collect their benefit. They don't have to pay themselves the payments you defaulted on. All they experience is a temporary cessation of payments that were supposed to have been made by you, which is offset by the value of the assets they repossess. They view the cost of carrying your property in the interim as simply the cost of doing business. It's just an entry in a ledger. Never mind the suffering and damage done to your family and community.

Once the deflationary cycle has run its course and the inflation begins again, the Dominators who took your home will make another loan on your property, to the next buyer, with money created from nothing. If they booked a paper loss on your loan so much the better, they can deduct that amount on their taxes. You don't get to claim a tax deduction for your loss, and in some cases the federal government will tax you for "debt forgiveness" as if it were income.

Then, the Dominators will sell your home or business to the next person making massive interest on the new loan which will more than cover any losses they experienced by your default. They may even recoup the amount of the original loan plus a percentage of the equity that was once your life savings. Bonus! Then the whole cycle begins anew. Again, it is more complicated than that but the principles behind the foregoing story run true. This is how the Dominators make money on both the In Breath and the Out Breath which means they always make money using the secret money system no matter what is happening.

The Fourth Item in the Dominator agenda is: *Position yourself to make money on both the inflationary and deflationary cycles.*

In the United States there have been approximately 47 recessions since 1790. That's about one every 5 years. It would be highly naive to think such a regular event cascade wasn't intentional. Do recessions happen because working families have somehow fallen down in their desire or ability to be productive at work? That is not the case.

Recessions are the result of self indulgent feeding frenzies created by the Dominators that severely alter economic balances, effecting our currency and economy in negative ways, purely for personal profit.

If we are going to stop that mechanism from wreaking havoc upon us all we will have to re-examine who is allowed to control our financial system and why they are allowed to have control.

CHAPTER NINE

Let's Go To War

When the processes of inflation and deflation have become exhausted from overuse there is always the third and final option for stimulating economic growth. The In Breath and the Out Breath have caused such economic chaos, there is sure to be someone who is sufficiently offended to be willing to fight over it. Since Dominator businesses are multi-national, they live above the political fray and manipulate it for their own advantage. Going to war to stimulate certain economic activities is a very old game. The strategy of war that follows represents a general pattern that has been used in conflict after conflict by all of the major players on the world stage. The United States has used this pattern in one country after another. We call it spreading democracy.

It may be difficult for the average working person to comprehend that a Dominator with massive capital can buy a large position in a publicly traded company almost at will. If they can cause that market to accelerate then they "make" a lot of money. Causing markets to accelerate or decelerate by manipulating market forces is now standard operating procedure on the world financial stage. One very common historical device used by the Dominators to accelerate market forces is war.

Let's say there haven't been any wars lately, since the Dominators have been busy inflating the economy of the homeland. The Dominators have kept the easy credit window open for too long, the homeland currency is staggering under the burden and is about to collapse. The population is starting to smell a rat and is growing uneasy. Political protests like Occupy Wall Street are taking place and Dominator profits from the inflationary cycle have peaked and are slowing.

As a result of the short period of peace that occurred while the Dominators pumped fake money into a growing economy, the stock price of companies that produce weapon systems, munitions and military supplies are slightly depressed from previous levels, due to reduced sales activity. Now is a good time to buy. So the Dominators buy a large position in the munitions industry at a favorable price. The next step is to establish an external threat to the security of the homeland.

A problem has arisen in a particular foreign country. Low and behold, a certain dictator has gone off the reservation and is making noise about death to the capitalist imperialists. Said dictator has committed certain atrocities and crimes against humanity, as dictators sometimes do. Said dictator also has certain natural resources at his disposal that could be used to finance a holy war against the capitalist unbelievers.

Let's say in this case he possesses oil. In a feeble attempt to mount a future holy war against the capitalist enslavers our dictator has assembled a meager supply of various weapon systems that were in fact manufactured by the capitalist imperialists during the last conflict and were previously sold to our dictator as surplus. Now, all of a sudden those weapons of mass destruction represent a suspiciously convenient threat to the security of the homeland.

If we go to war now, the additional economic stimulus of preparing for war might actually pull the domestic currency system back from the brink of destruction, cure the overfeeding condition and allow the Dominator's charade to continue for a while. There will be an added bonus as we send our troops off to extinguish the serious external threat. There is nothing like a righteous war to take the population's attention away from certain domestic economic issues.

So, the Dominators tell the politicians, "We must do the right thing. Send in the troops now." Off we go into the wild blue yonder, land on the shores of our errant dictator (who actually does deserve to be deposed) and commence killing people and destroying infrastructure in defense of freedom and democracy. This effort is paid for by the people of the homeland and costs the Dominators nothing.

The media (which is owned by the Dominators) fills the airwaves with the true and noble stories of the heroism of our soldiers who are being maimed and are sacrificing their lives for the homeland. Meanwhile, in order to supply the effort to put things right, the politicians (who are owned by the Dominators) have instructed the government to spend massive amounts of the people's money on sweetheart deals with the munitions and military supply companies (owned by the Dominators) in a valiant attempt to quell the threat to the homeland.

Our politicians have been willing to use the people's money to fund enormous profit taking in the private sector. Politicians, it turns out, can be bought rather cheaply when compared to the largesse of the treasury they are capable of handing out.

Having shifted their focus from inflating the economy to making war, the Dominators are taking in substantial profits once again. After a suitable period of destruction of roads, bridges, buildings and other forms of infrastructure the errant dictator is brought to justice and removed from power. The Dominators are now in control of the dictator's country but they have some bad press to deal with. Our news channels are screaming that the government used the excuse of weapons of mass destruction to gain control of the oil or other natural resources.

"Not at all," say the Dominators, "We will demonstrate our good faith by restoring the oil fields, re-establishing the revenue stream and we will place the proceeds in the new central bank of the conquered country to be used to rebuild the country on behalf of its people. We will establish democracy for the benefit of all." The Dominators proceed to do just that, sort of.

The Dominators have already made massive profits supplying the munitions required to destroy the country. What happens next is the Dominators hire companies (owned by them) to restore the oil fields damaged during the great and noble war, who will be paid with proceeds of the future sale of oil. This is spun as a humanitarian effort since the oil field companies are willing to begin construction prior to re-establishing the revenue stream that will be the method of payment for their services.

Next, the Dominators ship the oil using tanker companies (owned by them) that transport the oil to retail companies (owned by them) in the homeland. This process yields a reciprocal benefit to the politicians, who called for war in the first place, since oil supplies are secured and the price of gas at home declines slightly.

Next, having restored the oilfield revenue stream, the Dominators establish a new central bank (controlled by them) to receive the funds from the sale of oil to the homeland, which will be used to rebuild the country they caused to be destroyed in the first place. This is spun as another humanitarian gesture toward the people of the conquered country. We are, after all, helping them to establish the freedom of democracy in their backward country. In a series of non-competitive backroom sweetheart deals with huge construction conglomerates, (owned by the Dominators) the long term rebuilding of the country commences and is paid for (on behalf of the conquered people) with the oil revenues that have been placed in the new central bank. It's great to be a builder!

Next, the central bank issues a new fractional reserve currency (created out of nothing) that will be used to conduct the country's domestic transactions. The Dominators have just been paid handsomely every step of the way to establish the first item on the Dominator agenda—gain control of the currency and establish Fractional Reserve Banking as the law of the land. The Dominators then open new retail banks and credit card companies with which to serve the needs of the people by helping to grow the economy.

Let the lending begin!

To sweeten the deal even further, the entire operation cost the Dominators nothing because, with the blessing of our government, the whole effort to conquer the country was paid for with tax money supplied by the people of the homeland. The people of the homeland, who are now even further into a growing national debt, (owed to the Dominators) than they were before. There is nothing for the people to complain about since the cost of the operation falls under the defense budget of the homeland, and has been expected all along. We all know that's what we have to do to defend our *freedom.* Anything less is unpatriotic.

Finally, the Dominators make another bundle selling their positions in the companies that manufactured the munitions to prosecute the war at a handsome profit due to elevated stock values resulting from the increased sales activity in war munitions. As military activity winds down and the stock price softens, that profit will be paid for by hoards of less sophisticated investors, who don't understand the Dominator Agenda, and who bought in at the peak thinking the trend toward military expansion would continue.

We, the people, get sent to war to defend the idea of freedom, we so cherish, that is being systematically eroded by the people who are sending us to war.

Breathe In, Breathe Out. War is good for business. Not to worry, after the stock price softens due to a temporary lull in military activity, the Dominators will buy back their positions in the munitions companies at a reduced price just in time for the next conflict.

The Fifth Item in the Dominator Agenda is: *Buy the government by dispensing campaign contributions and promising lucrative future employment in return for the largesse of the treasury.*

Misguided or not, do you still wonder why capital-ism has earned a bad reputation in certain parts of the world? When foreign countries refer to American Imperialism they are referring to the activities of the American Aristocracy of Capital.

Author's Note: I want to be clear that I support our troops with all my heart and abhor the sacrifices they make with their bodies and their lives. I pray that when the final analysis comes, after the passing of the Dominator Era, we will have some real freedoms left to defend. We should honor the sacrifices of our military men and women by making the cultural changes that are needed to ensure that the freedom they paid for with their lives is worthy of being defended. Profits for Dominators is not a worthy trade for the lives of our loved ones.

CHAPTER TEN

The Fully Amortized Loan

In previous chapters we discussed how the shift from an equity based economy to a debt service economy took place after World War II and what some of the consequences have been. The Dominators have created a playbook of devices they have used to gain control of the worldwide financial system and operate it for their own benefit while both the inflationary and ecological costs are paid for by the rest of us. One of the most prolific devices the Dominator's have used to establish the present level of worldwide indebtedness is the fully amortized loan.

To study this device, let's use the example of a $300,000.00 fully amortized, fixed rate, thirty year home mortgage at 6 percent interest, which is roughly the average interest rate I have paid on the five homes I have owned during the last thirty years. (Interest rates are somewhat lower as I write this, but few can take advantage of them because credit requirements have tightened as a result of the recent crash. Not to worry, interest rates will go back up soon and then you will be able to borrow again and buy your next home at the higher rate.)

A loan is considered to be fully amortized if at the end of its term, when all scheduled payments have been made, both the interest and the principle are paid off in full. Our sample loan consists of 360 equal monthly payments of $1,798.65. The interest rate of six percent is fixed so the monthly payment remains fixed as well. Each monthly payment consists of an amount paid for interest and an amount paid toward reducing the debt. While the monthly payment remains the same, the percentage of the payment used for interest charges and the percentage of the payment used to actually retire the debt vary widely over the years of the loan.

What you may not be aware of is that fully amortized loan interest is heavily front loaded. The financial system's rationale for this is that you owe more principal at the beginning of the loan and therefore should pay more interest on the outstanding balance. That rationale fades when you realize the money you have borrowed cost nothing to create in the first place. At the end of the loan you owe less principal and therefore should pay less interest. The following chart shows how those amounts charged to interest and principal vary in 6 year increments for this loan.

	Monthly payment	Amount paid in interest	Amount paid in principal	Loan balance
Payment 1	1,798.65	1,500.00	298.65	299,701.35
Payment 72	1,798.65	1,373.10	425.55	274,193.86
Payment 144	1,798.65	1,189.24	609.41	237,238.32
Payment 216	1,798.65	925.95	872.71	184,238.32
Payment 288	1,798.65	548.90	1,249.75	108,529.76
Payment 360	1,798.65	8.95	1,789.70	00.00

On the face of it, the above chart seems like it could be fair. As time goes by, more and more money is applied to the principal of the loan. However, I'd like to draw your attention to Payment 72. The reason I divided the payment chart into six year increments is that according one statistical website, the median length of time a person kept a mortgage between 2001 and 2008 was six years.[6]

After six years of ownership, our home owner has either refinanced or sold his home and is starting the front-loaded interest clock all over again on the next loan. After having made 72 payments during the first six years, our home owner has reduced his principal by only 25,806 dollars but has paid a whopping 103,696 dollars in interest in return for the privilege of ownership (meaning that our homeowner also gets to pay for property tax and maintenance as well.)

That means for every dollar our home buyer actually paid toward the loan balance on his home, he also paid 4 dollars in interest. Judging by the number of these loans being issued, we would conclude that society at large has agreed that this confiscation of wealth is fair. Or maybe the market is rigged?

Well, you say, not moving is a much better financial plan so you can take advantage of the interest curve in the last years of your mortgage. Fine, if you want to, or are even capable of staying in the same home for 30 years. But, as we all know, we have different housing requirements as young parents with children than we do as senior citizens. Almost everyone goes through job changes during their career that may require a move. Maybe you don't like the way your old neighborhood is deteriorating. Maybe you want to move to a different climate. Maybe you are doing well financially and can afford a nicer home.

Every time you change loans you start the interest clock all over again. If you were to move 5 times in 30 years to identically priced houses, were able to transfer your equity without loss from one home to the next, and had the same loan as the above example on each home, after 30 years you would reap the following result: You will have paid only 129,000 dollars toward the principal of your 300,000 dollar loan, you will still owe

171,000 dollars on your current home and you will have paid $518,480 dollars in interest on your various real estate loans. We are not even taking into account the 90,000 dollars you paid in 6% real estate commissions for the sale of the five homes you lived in over the last 30 years. Let's not even mention the loan origination, appraisal, inspection and other fees associated with each new loan! That's freedom right?

The income streams generated by these loans are so massive Wall Street has bundled them as securities and sold them to investors. You may want to ask why capital that was originally created from nothing has the ability to command such an outrageous percentage of a working family's earnings? Is this a natural law of some kind or the result of a belief system imposed from the top down?

Slowly we are starting to understand who the people are that have the power to impose such a system on society. The goldsmith story showed that the creation of money as debt imposes an economic burden upon all users of a currency while the benefits of that system accrue to a very small group in control of the monetary system.

If common folks ultimately bear the economic burden of money created as debt then it stands to reason they should receive the benefits of the interest charged on it. But that isn't how the system works, is it?

CHAPTER ELEVEN

Free Markets? Really?

If we coin a word to represent someone or something and it becomes a term in popular use, does the way it is used in daily practice actually change the meaning of the word over time? I believe it does. For example, the terms "making money" and "earning money" used to mean the same thing. The definition of earning money is still relatively unchanged. To earn, means to deserve just compensation for acts of merit that create value and contribute to the well being of society. To earn, means to add value by engaging in acts of creativity. On the other hand the term "making money" has now changed.

You might have noticed in the past, the average working person and the people who run the secret money system both referred to the activity of acquiring money as "making money." However, there is now a vast difference between the two activities. In "making money," acts of merit are no longer considered to be essential. The average salaried or hourly worker is paid money in return for creating value. Value is generated by combining raw materials with labor and creativity to produce goods or by providing labor directly as a service to the buyer. For most people, that is what it means to ***earn money.***

You can easily see that the practitioners of the secret money system do not create value or engage in acts of merit on behalf of society. They confiscate value from those who create it, both through inflation of the currency and the interest charged on money created from nothing, along with hundreds of other techniques. They don't *"earn money"* so much as they *"make money"* on the backs of the general population.

The bad news is, these are the people we have traditionally held in high regard as the pinnacle of human achievement. The really sneaky part is that they have designed a covert system to drain a little bit of real value from everyone who uses their paper money, all the time, and so gradually that the populace at large is unaware of what is happening to them. Even if they are aware, they have no idea what to do about it.

Way too many people have been persuaded that receiving money for business activities that have no real and lasting merit to society, is a legitimate way to make a living. In today's world, jobs that literally confiscate wealth from people, pay well and are coveted positions. Wall Street is a perfect example of that trend. In today's lexicon, the definition of the term "making money" has been changed by the Dominators to mean literally making it out of nothing or confiscating it from others.

When I was a youngster, the words *"free enterprise"* and *"capitalism"* meant the same thing. They were used interchangeably in the common culture. Free enterprise hasn't changed all that much. To be free of restriction is still recognized as a virtue by all freedom loving souls. However, don't we each have a responsibility to make sure we don't soil the deeper meaning of the term, and destroy its integrity, by using our freedom to restrict the freedom of other humans with the same rights?

If we do that frequently, then the meaning of *"free enterprise"* changes into one of *the privilege of freedom for the few*

who are capable of taking systemic advantage of others. The word *"capitalism"* spoken at the grass roots level used to mean a system in which any person had the freedom to earn and save up enough capital to start a small business for themselves with the possibility that it could grow into something highly successful.

Every person was supposed to have the right to pursue their version of the American Dream any way he or she could afford, so long as they remained within the law and the boundaries of morality. We can still do that, but only in an environment that is heavily and covertly restricted by the Dominator Agenda.

During my lifetime, having the freedom and opportunity to work hard and create a small business that would provide for one's family has been the ideal of the American Dream. Most small business people understand that the path to success is to be honest with one's customers and to produce real value. Historically we have called that Capitalism.

On the other hand, the merciless activities of Wall Street bankers, brokers and speculators that led to sub-prime financing, the explosive inflation of the housing market, the global financial crisis and the foreclosure upon millions of working class Americans, is also referred to as Capitalism. These bankers, brokers and speculators walked away with hundreds of billions of dollars. Very few were ever prosecuted for their crimes against society.

How can we use the same word to describe such very different activities? Capitalism at the Wall Street level means to shower monetary benefits of every description on the holders of capital. The more capital you have, the more you are able to command special influence in every area of life. The people in the limousines appear to be willing to cut the throats of every middle class working family to get what they want, and we still seem to hold them in high regard.

The activities of earning a living by creating real value for others versus making money by buying low and selling high are so different that we owe it to ourselves to label them differently. Earning a living by creating real value should now be referred to as:

Honest Free Enterprise.

Making money by market manipulation, speculation and financial sleight of hand is what *Capital-ism* has become. That definition could be rehabilitated if the people who proudly call themselves capitalists would, by their own actions, cause the original meaning to re-emerge into the common parlance. Don't hold your breath.

Before you jump on your high horse and declare me to be a communist or socialist, please listen carefully to what I am saying. I want honest free enterprise. That is not what we have today or what we refer to as Capital-ism.

Capitalists continually testify that the natural law of supply and demand will deliver economic justice for us all. Free markets did that once upon a time and could still do so again if they actually were free markets. But, the Dominators, while touting the sanctity of free markets, are at the same time doing everything humanly possible to rig every one of those so called free markets to their own advantage. They have hired legions of computer experts to help them do it.

They have been so fabulously successful at it, there is no longer anything resembling legitimate price discovery driven by true competition in a free market. The result of these nefarious activities is that prices are no longer set by the law of supply and demand. They are set by market leverage, manipulation and monopoly. When that is allowed to happen, the law of supply and demand is rendered impotent and cannot deliver any benefit to society.

The natural laws of the free market, which we believed would provide economic justice for all, have been corrupted from the inside out. The natural laws of the free market that we thought we were building our culture upon have been destroyed by the very people who tout them as the foundation of a free democratic society.

The Sixth Item in the Dominator Agenda is: *Rig every market you are capable of influencing for your own benefit.*

There are a lot of folks who think the only alternatives for political and social organization are capitalism, socialism, communism or fascism and that of these the best system ever created is capitalism. I agree, that so far capitalism has been the best system for stimulating the production and sale of goods.

However, as the results of the latest cycle have demonstrated, we don't really own those goods free and clear because we borrowed the money to buy them. This process has resulted in massive un-payable debts for individuals, companies and nations. We can do better than that and still be free. Unfortunately, the paradigm under which capitalism has been built dictates that it will self implode if growth stops.

We stand on the threshold of the realization that the tremendous economic growth of the last 50 to 60 years has been created by borrowing from the future and the bill is finally coming due.

If you are critical of capitalism, you risk being painted as un-American and you will be declared to belong to one of the other three camps. I couldn't disagree more! There are other alternatives we desperately need to recognize. Whether they live in communist countries or in the west, working people all over the world are now realizing that they simply want ***honest free enterprise***. They want to be paid an honest living wage for their work without fear that the wealth they have stored, will be confiscated in the future. They want to keep what they earn.

None of us want to stand by helplessly as the Dominators remotely destroy our jobs, from far away ivory towers, while pursuing unearned profits in leveraged buyouts, the exportation of domestic jobs to foreign shores, and other forms of economic manipulation. Working people everywhere want genuine free enterprise. The words, ***"free enterprise"*** have been soiled but can still be saved. Now it's time to separate free enterprise from capitalism. They are no longer synonymous. The concept of free enterprise has been used by the Dominators as permission to employ their freedom to tap or harness the freedom of others.

The Dominator Agenda has artificially stimulated the growth of immature technologies that have upset the balance of the natural systems we rely on for our survival. I say immature technologies, because businesses spawned by the Dominator Agenda haven't been designed to exist in harmony with the ecology of our planet and are not sustainable over the long term.

Air quality is a symptom of that lack of wisdom. It is widely accepted that the machines and processes we have created to fuel the growth of material consumption have degraded air quality to the point where it is effecting global weather patterns. A growing segment of the population believes those patterns are now on a path to endangering the future of human life.

The Dominator Agenda ultimately destroys that which it creates in order to extract the last drop of value from others for its own account. Unfortunately we may have to watch as the parasites destroy the host for their own short term gratification. We may have to watch as the Dominators destroy the world's financial system in a final futile attempt to have what they believe will satisfy them.

The really sad thing is, like the drug addict that needs the short term gratification of the heroin which is actually destroying his or her life, the Dominator Belief System is so primitive and so short sighted it can't stop itself from committing suicide, out of sheer arrogance, in the willful pursuit of material gratification. When the Dominator Agenda finally goes up in a blaze of glory we will all be affected by it in ways we don't yet fully understand.

Energy Carries Intention: Dominators recognize that money is a form of energy. What they don't seem to understand is, energy carries intention.

When energy is obtained by greed and insensitivity to the suffering of others, it will manifest that same vibration in the lives of those who obtained it that way, whether they recognize it or not.

If you are a dedicated materialist you will think that comment is just superstitious nonsense, or you might consider that statement to be of religious origin. You will discover in the near future that it is a law of quantum physics.

When you create massive suffering by stealing the energy of other sentient beings, it doesn't matter what you acquire with the energy you confiscated, you will not be able to buy the peace and happiness you so deeply desire with it. You can't because energy carries the intention you used to acquire it. You might become wealthy, you might be admired for your collection of material goods, but you will not be able to quench the deepest yearning of your soul to be fulfilled.

Dominators are convinced that it's a dog eat dog world and you must take what you want from others or they will take it from you. Those who continue to engage in this philosophy, also continue to prove that we live in a world where it is still true. They don't appreciate the value in creating a world where everyone is encouraged from birth to be vital, creative, intelligent and artistic and to walk the earth in peace.

They don't believe in the synergistic reward of large numbers of creative people collectively designing a new future based upon benevolence and an innate respect for other humans. Do you want to live in a world where almost everyone has a deep respect for and belief in the creative capabilities of all humans acting together to make a better world for all? I do.

The deepest yearning of your soul can be quenched through selfless acts of kindness and support for other human beings, not through graft and manipulation. However, once you really understand that you can't go back, your days as a Dominator are numbered.

CHAPTER TWELVE

The Pattern Is Repeated

In the preceding chapters I outlined not only a belief system, but a process used by the Dominators for gaining control of most of the social systems and nearly all of the monetary systems which are used to run the affairs of humanity. The belief system behind the Dominator Agenda is being used in business model after business model around the world. There are thousands of plays in the Dominator Playbook and I'd like to cover just a few more very quickly. Then we'll move on to other topics. Rather than belabor the point to death by devoting a chapter to each one, I'll just summarize a few more of those business models to build a sense of how pervasive the Dominator Agenda is.

Dominators are the essence of central control. They want to be at the center, controlling all of the social and monetary systems that run the planet. They are having a competition to see who the winners will be. You may have noticed that big companies are gobbling up smaller companies. Our politicians and financial people are trying to create one economic union after another. The logical outcome of massive political and economic centralization is to concentrate absolute power into fewer and fewer hands.

The downside of that trend is that we will then be saddled with the morality of the group who has used the method of co-erced subjugation to achieve its end game. It would seem that a better way to create a new world would be to de-centralize as much as possible. Then, we will return social and economic control to a wider and wider network of people who are held responsible for what they do at the local level by the people they actually interact with on a daily basis.

Dominators believe they are the pinnacle of human achievement. I used to wonder—what would have happened if Hitler had won World War II? The answer that keeps popping up is, he might have conquered the world, but he wouldn't have been able to administrate it once he did. The Third Reich was based upon a totally unsustainable paradigm. The Third Reich was supposed to generate a society in which the master race was to be in charge of everyone else. It was touted as being the reality of the next 1,000 years. It really only lasted 12 years!

Hitler was defeated by the energy, creativity, enthusiasm and sacrifice of common Americans and Europeans. I believe the paradigm that runs the Dominator empire is also not sustainable, it's starting to crumble. The evidence is surfacing all around us. There are big changes about to be demanded by common American citizens to protect and redefine what it means to be an American.

Following are some of the business models that will need to change to make a new world possible:

Healthcare: There is only one reason the cost of healthcare is skyrocketing to the current level. That reason is the attractive profits being accumulated at the top of the healthcare monetary food chain by a very few people. You may have noticed that individual medical practices are being assimilated into larger and larger conglomerates. Our western medical system is not about healing people by addressing the root causes of disease. It is about the cash flow that is created by the long term treatment of symptoms. At the same time healthcare costs are going up, doctor's pay is going down. That makes for increased profits for whom? The entire healthcare system has been designed according to the Dominator Agenda to funnel massive funds from both the public and the government into the hands of a few at the top of both the healthcare and insurance industries. In America your participation is mandatory. They want to control and manipulate you for profit.

Big Pharma: 70% of Americans have one prescription they pay for monthly. 50% of Americans have more than one. The average cost of prescription drugs per capita in the U.S. hovers around $1,000.00 per year. Multiply that by the current population and you can see that the prescription drug business in the U.S. is worth approximately 319 billion dollars per year give or take a few billion.

How often do you go to see your doctor about an ailment and don't come away with a prescription? Seldom, in my experience. The drug companies arrange for your doctor to receive certain benefits in return for prescribing their products. They watch his performance carefully to make sure he is doing his best to promote their wares. Big Pharma relies on the patent process to create mini drug monopolies that allow it to employ confiscatory pricing policies of up to 5,000 percent profit for single source drugs, for a 20 year period after they are approved.

The same drugs are available from the same companies at lower prices in other countries. That is because prices are not set as a function of the cost of labor and materials plus a reasonable mark up for profit. The cost of pharmaceutical drugs is set according to how the market for medicine can be rigged. One big pharma executive was recently arrested for securities fraud. The ensuing investigation revealed he had also increased the price of a decades old drug used to treat a life threatening parasitic condition by 5,500 percent. Allegedly, he needed to rob the coffers of his pharmaceutical company to pay for substantial losses he incurred at a hedge fund he managed. That kind of piggish morality is all too common in the pharmaceutical industry. They want to control and manipulate you for profit.

GMO Companies: The GMO companies have one objective, to replace the natural biosphere with genetically modified plant material that can be patented so those plants can be owned. They want to control the seed and pesticide markets for our entire plant based food supply. The Dominators have set up their business plan so the purchasers of GMO seeds are prohibited from raising seed themselves and must buy new seed from them every year in order to continue growing their engineered crops.

When the seed monopoly is finally established, all farmers will be at their mercy. There is a huge body of information that suggests that GMO's are not necessarily healthier for you and in fact may be highly dangerous in the long run. Tampering with nature may not produce the benefits they say they are selling. If GMO's are allowed to become the normal state of affairs, they may actually weaken the diversity of the biosphere and set us up for an unimaginable extinction event caused by overspecialization.

Over specialization occurs when you put all of your eggs in one basket and then are unable to respond to conditions you hadn't realized might arise as a result of your activities. The GMO companies want to use the patent process to create seed monopolies so they can employ confiscatory pricing policies for their seeds. They are attempting to rig the market for your food. They want to control and manipulate you for profit.

Credit Card Companies: The credit card companies lure you in with all sorts of ads showing deliriously happy people enjoying fabulous vacations in exotic lands. They promote reward schemes that will give you cash back, bonus points or frequent flyer miles. They extend zero percent interest for the first year and as much as 30% thereafter. You only pay interest if you don't pay the balance in full every month, but they make it easy for you to overspend. Then, you won't be able to pay in full every month and you will become a loyal blood (interest) donor to their cause. Why do credit card companies have the right to charge these unbelievable amounts of interest for the use of money that essentially cost them nothing to produce? They have that right because congress gave it to them. They want to control and manipulate you for profit.

Insurance Companies: The insurance industry provides products that protect you from catastrophic events related to your home, auto, life and health. They collect massive amounts of data about life expectancies, accident rates, theft rates, natural disasters and monetary exposures of all kinds. They compile that information into what are known as actuarial tables and use the information to set confiscatory pricing policies that ensure they make enormous profits all day every day. Insurance companies are some of the largest institutional investors.

You may have noticed that the bulk of claims you will ever make seem to fall below your deductable amount. Do you think that's a coincidence? Recently, my storage unit was broken into and the thieves stole a generator worth $950.00, my deductable was $1,000.00. The insurance industry knows the value of the average theft and sets rates that discourage you from having a lower deductable. Oh well, maybe they'll steal more next time. The insurance industry uses their statistical system to control and manipulate you for profit.

The Dominators Have Control: All of these devices and many more are intended to get you used to paying the Dominators on a monthly basis for monopolistic activities. These activities have been specially created to allow them to charge higher fees than could be expected from the same activity in truly competitive free markets. The best way to control a population is to control their money, their food, their fuel, their forms of communication and their healthcare. The Dominators already have control. Dominator control of everything, the overall theme behind the Dominator agenda, is the reason that worldwide wealth is so unequally distributed.

What would happen in our society if we successfully ended Dominator control?

CHAPTER THIRTEEN

Materialism And The Destruction Of Our Habitat

I want to add an additional concept that will help describe the Dominator belief system. Simply put, the Dominators we are concerned about are materialists. These are people for whom spiritual inquiry has largely ceased. If it hadn't ceased, we wouldn't be seeing one scheme after another to enslave innocent people for personal gain. Dominators worship the acquisition of material. They have created a pervasive culture that intends to seduce you into doing the same, though on a much smaller scale.

One of the more important characteristics of the material being worshiped is rarity. We have been asked to believe that rarity is synonymous with beauty and desirability. Dominators believe that being able to possess rare objects of desirable material beauty makes themselves rare and desirable by association. They believe the ownership of rare objects confers status upon them and they place a high value on status. They have demonstrated that they are willing to sacrifice their fellow humans and our planetary ecosystem in pursuit of status.

Van Gogh's painting, Starry Night, is an object of great and mysterious beauty. Being able to own that painting would confer considerable status upon the successful acquisitionist. The more expensive an object, the more exclusive it is and thus the more desirable it is to a Dominator. They believe that owning such objects is a self justifying activity and are willing to destroy both the environment and the lives of other people in order to have them.

In 1996 I turned away from commercial real estate. I really wanted to get into something more artistic. I established a small company that designed and built very expensive mansion interiors for a wealthy clientele in a well known ski town. One of my jobs was to integrate collections of very expensive art objects into the design of living space. For one client I designed and built a display shelf for five pre-Columbian pots worth over a million dollars. You can be sure I fastened it to the wall as securely as possible.

I spent quite a bit of time examining and planning for the display of art collections. During that time I discovered that there is a whole industry of art critics and appraisers whose job it is to make sure that an art object was genuinely one of a kind and could be traced to a particular artist or indigenous tribe. In other words there is an entire industry whose business it is to verify exclusivity.

While discussing the techniques for displaying various kinds of artifacts with my clients I learned that it wasn't just a delight in beauty that motivated them. Exclusivity was very important to them. It mattered that they were identified as belonging to an economic stratum that was able to acquire and own material objects that were available only to the holders of large amounts of capital and not to ordinary folks. They worshipped exclusivity along with the paradigm of materialism.

The Dominator Belief System is based upon one fundamental assumption: Everything that is worthwhile to obtain in life exists outside of you.

Dominators place value upon owning material that others cannot afford. If they want to extol the value of an object, a restaurant or place to live, they will say that it is exclusive, meaning that it is available only to a few people at the top of the economic food chain with the good taste and the money to acquire it. If they were to hop in their Ferrari one morning and pull out onto the road, only to find that overnight a miracle had occurred and everyone else was driving Ferraris too, they would not be overjoyed at the good fortune of all the new owners. Part of the pleasure they feel by owning their highly priced car would be diminished because it lost its exclusivity.

Dominators like to surround themselves with the best materials. Part of my job was to be the one who knew where to acquire those materials, which materials to use and which craftsmen to hire. So, I became an expert in the best granite, the best tile, the best hardware, the best plumbing fixtures, the finest hand forged iron, the best wood species, as well as the techniques used to build fine cabinets and woodwork. I had to know all the options for covering walls in soft plaster, hard plaster, Venetian plaster and special faux painting techniques and textures. I made it my business to understand the best light fixtures and the best techniques for lighting living space and art objects. No client or supplier I was working with ever questioned our common motivation to create exclusivity. We all strove to come up with the most exclusive and creative way to display the trappings of wealth.

Occasionally, my wife and I would be asked to travel with a client and their family to another of the many homes they owned to consult on what might be done in that location. Necessarily we became a part of that family's social life for a short time. We attended parties at the homes of our client's friends and associates. Invariably our role as the purveyors of good taste would encourage the host to take us on a tour of their exclusive stuff, its provenance, and the techniques that had been employed to display and light it.

I became a serious aficionado of material goods I could not afford to own. When you spend your day supervising the installation of a delicately curved staircase with a wood and hand-forged iron balustrade that cost over $100,000 and then return home to your staircase with the spindles from Home Depot, the contrast is not lost upon you. I wasted a lot of years desiring what I thought I wanted, but would never be able to have. It took years for me to understand what I was really looking for.

During the inflationary bubble of the 1990's I was referred from one client to another without ever placing an ad for my firm's services. Most of our projects were conducted on a cost plus basis. On one such project the owner gave me a budget of $450,000 but then began adding more and more to the scope of work. I finally called a meeting with the client and told them that there was no way we were going to be able to come close to their budget. The man of the house laughed at me and said, "At this level, there is no such thing as a budget. Please, just produce the highest quality creative design and craftsmanship you are capable of and bill me for it."

We shook hands on it and he proceeded to spend $1,500,000 on his interior. I thought I died and went to heaven. I thought I finally had reached my pinnacle as a designer. There followed some very good years. But, true to form, like all inflationary cycles it would not last.

September 11th, 2001 changed everything. My clients were complaining about substantial losses they were incurring in the stock market. They cut back on spending. The contraction was sudden and violent. My business staggered for a couple of years before starting to come back. But something was different. People who had sung our praises years before were becoming harder and harder to please. If we produced a project that was 97% wonderful, they would concentrate on the 3% that wasn't quite up to their subjective expectations. This was something new. In the past, some of my wiser clients celebrated the little flaws that showed up here and there as the quality that made the difference between "handmade" and "mass produced" artifacts. I thought that was true wisdom.

We were the same company as before, and nothing we ever built was perfect, but some sort of perceptual malaise had descended upon our clientele. I confirmed that my colleagues in the business were having the same experience. We used to be able to create what I thought at the time, was happiness in our clients. But now, exactly the same activities were not producing those results any more. It was true across the board. People were not getting the same amount of pleasure from our work as they had in the late 90's. The paradigm was breaking down. I finally realized that we all had been riding another inflationary Dominator In Breath and it had come to a temporary end once again on 911.

Imagine my disappointment, I thought I had finally embodied my reason for being. I thought I had arrived at the pinnacle of my career as a purveyor of good taste and that the quality and cost of the material I was handling conferred status upon me. All of my clients were highly successful business people. As the inflationary cycle slowly ground to a halt and the Out Breath began, all of their businesses started shrinking and mine did as well. By the next crash in 2008 it was all over. I walked away from a paradigm I could no longer believe in.

I'm sure I have created the impression that I no longer approve of materialism at this level. It's not that I don't enjoy fine material or that there is something morally wrong with it. I loved working with beautiful materials. What I no longer believe in is the ability of that material to make any of us feel the higher emotions we so deeply desire to experience. The higher emotional frequencies of happiness, joy and genuine love are non-physical forms of energy that cannot be accessed through the material plane.

As we have heard over and over again, ***"You can't buy happiness."*** On the other hand if someone gave you a million dollars and told you to go attempt to buy happiness, who among us would refuse to give it the old college try? That answer is revealing isn't it.

What I did find to be true in my association with the ultra wealthy, is that you sure as hell can distract yourself from the really critical activity of self examination by having access to new stuff all the time. Wealth can distract you from paying attention to what is really important in life.

The flaws in the paradigm of the relentless pursuit of happiness through materialism are starting to stand out for more and more of us. The great cost to the planetary habitat of the lifestyle of highly successful materialists, is making itself readily apparent. The really dangerous aspect of this paradigm is that materialism has been presented to all classes of society as the true meaning of freedom.

Lifestyles of the rich and famous have been presented to modern culture as what we should want. The media tells us that we should make serious comprises in our value systems to obtain those lifestyles. We are continually being seduced by the glitz of materialism.

One lie that is constantly broadcast is that anyone who is willing to work hard can achieve the same high level of material success. Trust me, under the present system, it's only true in a few cases. If it were universally true, income distribution wouldn't be so heavily skewed. More of the general population would be wealthier. Another lie that is told over and over again is that the pursuit of materialism will quench the deepest yearning of your soul if you are successful at it. I'm not saying don't own nice things. I am saying, before you move mountains and enslave people to get what you ***think*** you want, ask yourself if it will make you ***feel*** the deepest level of satisfaction and peace that you really crave. That realization may be a tricky to assimilate since you have probably been raised in a culture that constantly disseminates the idea that materialism will deliver the peace and happiness you seek.

The business activities that embody the headlong rush to acquire more and more material objects, of higher and higher cost, constitute one of the most serious forces that are destroying the sacred habitat that we rely on for the survival of our species. Every industry that pollutes the land, air and water and that causes the wholesale destruction of our forests and wetlands has a group of Dominators at the top of its economic money trail. As a society we need to examine what we believe real value is. We need to examine the real reasons behind why we do what we do. The results we are generating are telling us that there is something wrong with our belief system.

When the end of life comes, the real value to be derived from having lived, is not measured by where we have been or by what we have possessed.

CHAPTER FOURTEEN

The Dominator Agenda
and
Its Belief System

It has been said that absolute power corrupts absolutely. History has demonstrated that the more power is concentrated in the hands of smaller groups of people, the higher the likelihood it will be used for some form of self indulgence. We should all be worried that the leaders of most of the governments and business empires on our planet subscribe to the primitive materialistic viewpoint that money, power, sex and status is the way to their true heart's desire. To quote a recent article in the Economist, "So extensive was the stash of jade, gold and cash found in the basement of General Xu Caihou's mansion in Bejing, that at least ten dump trucks were needed to haul it away."

As I write this, the supreme court of Brazil is investigating 50 sitting government officials for participating in a multi-billion dollar bribery scheme involving the state owned oil company Petrobras. It seems they all conspired to inflate construction contracts and received billions of dollars in kickbacks. The losses have forced the company to curtail its expansion plans resulting in the layoff of thousands of innocent workers and the destruction of many of the related businesses that served those workers. That scandal has helped plunge Brazil deeper into recession.

Similar stories are told around the world every week about those who wield power and have abused it for personal material gain, while destroying the lives of millions of working people. Similar stories abound about high ranking politicians and business people who have been seduced by the gaudy trappings of money, power, sex and status.

For an illuminating perspective on the pointlessness of the lifestyle oriented around power and materialism see the documentary movie "The Queen of Versailles". This film is about a couple who became paper billionaires in the real estate time-share business. In the movie, the purpose of their company is shown to be two fold. First, to develop luxury condominiums specifically for the time share market. Secondly, to manipulate the buying public into going into *debt* to purchase an annual week of occupancy in a luxury apartment so they can experience how it feels to be wealthy for a few days each year. Of course, the undeclared message is—fancy material goods make you happy, even if you can only pretend to own them for a little while.

The Seventh Item in the Dominator Agenda is*: Subjugate as many people as possible by manipulating them into debt to you.*

As an extension of their business plan, the couple's goal in their personal life is to build the biggest and fanciest house in the United States, based upon the palace at Versailles in France. The film follows the couple as they suffer through the global financial crisis of 2008, their business falters, and construction on their mega-home is halted. Since 2012 their resort business is back in the black and construction on the home has resumed while they celebrate their good fortune. The home is 90,000 square feet, which is about the size of a small shopping center.

It's so big they are planning to use Segway scooters to get around in it. What really stood out for me in watching this depiction of conspicuous consumption was that nobody seemed to question the premise behind it. Nobody asked, "Why are you doing this?" Nobody asked how this endeavor will contribute to the higher awareness or well being of its authors.

This project has been touted in popular culture as the pinnacle of the American Dream when it is really a fool's errand of the most egregious proportions. What it truly represents is the mindless paradigm, "More is Better." It is shocking to discover that such primitive value systems exist at the very top of the economic pyramid. However, I assure you that they do exist there and are being used on a daily basis to decide your fate.

The Dominator Agenda:

❖ *1. Gain control of a country's currency, make Fractional Reserve Banking the law of the land.*

❖ *2. Pump fake money into the system by loaning it as household debt.*

❖ *3. Pump fake money into the system by loaning it as governmental debt.*

❖ *4. Position yourself to make money on both the inflationary and deflationary cycles.*

❖ *5. Own the government, dispense campaign contributions in return for special treatment by politicians.*

❖ *6. Manipulate every market you are capable of influencing for your own benefit.*

❖ *7. Subjugate as many people as possible by manipulating them into debt to you.*

The intention of the Dominators is to develop and manifest a system that drains away energy from pretty much everyone and collects it all for their own benefit. They have been fabulously successful at it. They hide behind the machinations necessary to run such a system and call it "making a living." The truth is, despite the supposed glories of being surrounded by fantastically costly material goods, this system is scary, ignorant, dangerous, and anti-evolutionary in the extreme.

We are coming to a great crossroads in human history. The Dominator Agenda is destroying the ecosystems that humanity relies upon for its very existence. If the Dominator Agenda is allowed to continue there will undoubtedly be an involuntary disaster-driven reduction in the number of humans occupying our planet. This first mega-event, could result in the loss of tens or possibly hundreds of millions of people. It may occur as a reaction by nature to our collective lack of understanding the ecosystem of our own mother planet. It may occur as the war to end all wars. It will surely occur as the collapse of the anti-evolutionary and unsustainable financial system the Dominators have imposed upon our world. It will be a wake-up call for all of humanity.

In Parts I & II of this book, we established the concept that money is energy. What we should all object to is how an accumulation of energy in the hands of a very small and unaware number of people is being used to enslave rather than to empower. Dominators do not believe that the way to create a better world is to end subjugation in all its forms. Dominators do not believe that all humans should have the maximum freedom to express their individual free will. They do not believe real freedom would be good for us all. They don't want you creating new patterns of behavior that fall outside of their agenda. In the pursuit of what they have decided they want, the Dominators are willing to hold on to the old ways until it all implodes. When it does, they believe their capital will defend them. At that point, I'm not so sure money will be a great help to anyone. And, by the way, you can't end domination by becoming a bigger Dominator. We've already tried that. The methods and history of the Dominators suggest that they hold the following beliefs:

The Dominator Belief System:

- *Everything that is worthwhile to obtain in life exists outside of you, get more.*
- *We are all separate, what I do to you doesn't return to me.*
- *I am protected by my money.*
- *It's a dog eat dog world and you should take what you want from others before they take it from you.*
- *Having control of the flow of money is the only real freedom.*
- *You don't have to be concerned about producing real value on behalf of society.*
- *A fair price is whatever you can make a fully rigged and monopolized market bear.*
- *The earth is just a resource for us to exploit and plunder.*
- *To have the power to dominate the earth and the people on it is the ultimate goal in life.*
- *It's all about winning. Be a winner, the losers don't matter.*

Political Solutions? Do you believe we are going to create the new more egalitarian world we want through our political system? Are you struggling to decide which political leader represents the best hope for turning the Dominator Agenda into something we can all live with? I've been waiting for our political leadership to make those meaningful changes since the Kennedy Administration. The truth is, the Dominator Agenda has been operating in this country since its inception.

The founding fathers all knew about it. Jefferson, Franklin and Jackson all knew about it. While everything else has evolved in the last 240 years the Dominator Agenda forged ahead, gaining both monetary and technological strength. The system is now so out of balance it poses the greatest threat to the longevity of the human race that has ever existed.

One of the major problems is that the Dominators have bought the loyalty of most politicians as a condition for providing the funds necessary to put them in office. The Dominators do everything in their power to increase the cost of being elected, so potential candidates must come to them in order to finance their participation. In 2012 the cost of running a campaign for a house seat averaged 1.7 million dollars, the cost for a senate campaign averaged 10.5 million dollars and the cost for a presidential campaign exceeded one billion dollars. Do you really believe that kind of money is donated to our politicians with no strings attached?

As a result, our politicians are already compromised the day they take office. Unfortunately, the red versus the blue has become a scam argument to keep us all engaged while the men and women behind the curtain, assisted by their hired men and women in the US Congress, fleece you of your financial strength.

"In the US there is basically one party, the Business Party. It has two factions called Democrats and Republicans which are somewhat different but carry out variations on the same policies."
Noam Chomsky

The fractional reserve banking system promulgated by the central banks of the world always showers the benefits of the secret money system upon the holders of large amounts of capital while imposing the losses upon that segment of the population least able to shoulder the financial burden. That is why income inequality exists the way it does. As long as the fractional reserve banking system is allowed to continue, only a very small percentage of the world population will ever live their lives in a debt free condition. As long as the fractional reserve banking system is allowed to continue, the majority of governments will never be debt free.

It would be nice if we could turn to our political leaders and find real leadership there. It would be nice if they would recognize this system for what it is. But alas, unless there is a new crop of heroes poised to come forward, that we are as yet unaware of, there won't be a political solution. There won't be a political solution because the system makes sure that the people we send to Washington have been seduced by that system before they ever step into the halls of congress. They accomplish that by making sure our up and coming politicians are in debt to the Dominators in return for the prestige, lifetime pensions, exclusivity and largesse of political office.

They have been seduced by the siren song of materialism.

What is the ultimate control device used by humans to control other humans? Historically it has been force. Historically we went to war to solidify control over others. Slowly, through modern technology, we have been moving on to more subtle forms of control. Today, the most pervasive method we use to control others is **DEBT.** That debt is owed to the Dominators, who have willfully created our financial system to achieve the state of affairs wherein everyone on the planet is in debt to them.

It makes no difference whether economies are improving or imploding. It makes no difference whether those economies are capitalist, socialist or communist. The secret money system ensures that the Dominators make money and win in every country in which they are in control of the currency.

If you are in debt to someone else for the things you cherish, you are likely to do their bidding rather than to lose everything you have worked so hard for so long to accomplish. Under the Dominator Agenda, the kind of freedom we now have, is that we are free to decide *how* we will attempt to keep paying that debt. The freedom we have lost, for the most part, is the freedom to opt out of the Dominator Agenda, maintain a comfortable life style, and be debt free sovereign citizens.

We are now coming face to face with the realization that the growth rates of one national economy after another have been achieved, not through honest free market forces but through artificially created financial stimulation in the form of debt. That debt and the interest on it is now growing so fast it threatens to consume personal, and national budgets all over the world. At the same time, corporations, whose management systems are based upon the Dominator Agenda, are awash in cash. If you are looking you will see these conditions clearly in the international financial news.

The growth rates of the last 60 years, that we have come to think of as a result of the American Dream having gained acceptance around the world, have been achieved in very large measure by borrowing from the future.

The bill is coming due and it will not be paid by the Dominators at the top of the worldwide Ponzi scheme. The Dominators intend for that bill to be paid by everyone else. Individuals, companies and governments now find themselves in debt to a very small segment of the population at levels never before known or experienced on this planet. Like a clothes washer on spin cycle, that is out of balance, the thumping of the Dominator based financial system is beginning to be heard around the world.

There won't be a political solution because the Dominators own the political systems. How will we create a new world that favors the success of average people if the people have no political voice? Fortunately the Dominator Agenda is beginning to come apart of its own accord. The curtain is falling away and the people who hide behind it are being exposed. The world population is now educated enough for a majority to understand what has really been done and why things are the way they are.

We will create a new world by changing the culture that we live in. We will change the culture we live in by changing who we are and what we believe, one person at a time. At the heart of that change will be a shift in who our heroes are. We will turn away from admiring people for the material goods they possess and the glitzy status they have enjoyed. Materialism is losing its allure. A new wisdom tradition is emerging.

At the heart of that new wisdom tradition is the understanding that we are all connected at the most fundamental level. What I do to you, I eventually do to myself. What has changed in the modern world is the rate of speed at which what I do to you comes back to me.

Are you willing to take unfair physical or monetary advantage of other human beings for your own personal material gain?

All of the foregoing knowledge motivates me to answer the Dominator question with a resounding,

"No Thank You."

PART III

The American Spirit

CHAPTER FIFTEEN

A Letter From The Future

The Greenstone Community,
Territory of Montana, June 21st, 2050

Dear Friends in the Southland,

I was awakened by bird song at 5:00 AM this morning, as I am every day at this time of the year. The morning twilight is under way and the birds sound happy. Most mornings the clouds turn orange and pink and the sky becomes bright long before the sun peeks over the mountains. It's going to be another mega-beautiful summer day.

You folks in the lower latitudes may not know that our wonderful summer days here are 18 hours long. As we approach the summer solstice, the morning sun rises and sets at a steep angle against the horizon causing the most delicious, prolonged periods of twilight at both sunrise and sunset. The quality of the light on the mountains during these times is something to experience rather than describe. I suppose every place has something unique to recommend it. This morning I'm taking some time just to sit and reflect on the events that gave us the world we live in and the sacrifices of those who made it possible.

My grandfather passed away last fall. He was 101 years old. That's not really extraordinary these days, though I understand it once was. Everyone keeps saying 100 is the new 80. Last month I went through his remaining possessions. He left me his saddle and his Winchester rifle. I discovered a box of paperbacked books he wrote back in the twenties, right after the second great depression. I've been reading them every morning. He was born a century ago in 1949, if you can imagine such a thing. His father actually fought in World War Two. The changes that occurred during his lifetime were so amazing you wonder how they all took the strain of it. When he was a boy there was no such thing as climate change, space travel or computers.

He grew up in a small mid-west town. He realized, as a young man, that he was uncomfortable with what passed for civilization in those days. Some historians refer to the second half of the 20th century as the age of specialization. Everyone was supposed to go to school and then college, pick out the job they wanted and stay in that career for most of their lives. Gramps was a generalist even back then. He never wanted to be a specialist, he wanted to understand as much of the big picture as possible.

Gramps began his career as a builder. In the early 1980's he worked his way up to being a corporate executive in the commercial real estate development industry. He built over a million square feet of old style shopping centers. Being in the development business allowed him to look behind the curtain and understand how the leviathan known as 20th century California came into being. For a few years he had access to a succession of company airplanes and flew around the west a lot. He said he had seen so much of the west from 10,000 feet he could hold a picture of it in his mind. He mentioned to me that he was profoundly influenced by seeing so much of the west from the air.

This was before global climate change started. He understood roads, bridges, traffic movement, structural engineering and even what was known in those days as financing. He knew where the water and power came from and where the sewage went because he managed the engineers who designed and built the facilities needed to serve the developments he worked on. He worked with city governments and planning commissions to get his developments approved. Being a generalist, he was a student of the forces that were creating civilization.

Right after World War II Americans fell in love with the automobile. You've all seen the pictures. They were nothing like the trans-pods we have now. The automobile was considered to be the pinnacle of freedom. You could get in your car and go anywhere you wanted. It was a symbol of freedom. It must have been intoxicating.

Anyway, they began to design everything they built around delivery trucks and automobiles. Because driving was so inexpensive they could separate noisy commercial activity from the places in which they had their homes. They lived in one place and shopped and went to work in completely separate places many miles away.

In the beginning it was considered to be a privilege to be able to drive across town every day. But the more California grew, the more crowded it got. Eventually, they had giant traffic jams where hundreds of thousands of cars would creep along at 2 mph for hours at a time. What was once considered to be a pleasure turned into a necessity that wasn't much fun anymore. The more people traveled back and forth every day, the more the environment suffered. Nobody in power opposed the reason everyone was migrating all over town in the first place. They just kept accommodating the automobile. That pattern was being repeated in countries around the world and was ultimately mistaken for freedom.

Once upon a time, America had unified agrarian communities like we do now, but the automobile changed everything. People in general became separated from each other. They created these giant developments called suburbs where they went at the end of the day to eat and sleep before getting back in their cars to drive across town to where they worked during the week. In those days they bought all their food which was grown far away and trucked into what were known as "supermarkets." Gramps said that during that time, the average meal came from 1,500 miles away. Most of that food wasn't grown by farmers, it was formulated by chemists and manufactured in giant food processing plants.

The automobile caused society to break down, in a very quiet way, as people stopped having reasons to relate to their neighbors. In those vast suburbs no one had cooperative economic relationships with each other. They no longer depended upon the cooperation of their neighbors to live or to survive in a crisis. They all traveled somewhere else to be in work relationships with people they didn't live with. They all got in their cars and went somewhere else for almost everything. In fact you could live within a quarter mile of thousands of people and not really know any of them in a deeper way. That was considered to be normal. How's that for strange?

They actually separated their homes from any kind of manufacturing or agriculture. Everything became centralized. Instead of the decentralized high tech mini plants and growing facilities we have now, they created huge factories where thousands of people would arrive in their cars every day and all the raw materials would be trucked into the same place. The noise and the pollution were terrific.

They removed the activity of making things from the environment where their kids grew up. You could no longer go down the street and observe people making clothes or tools or anything at all for that matter. Generations of people forgot how to make things for themselves. Americans started to believe their labor was too costly to suffer the indignity of making anything. So, they shifted all of their manufacturing ability overseas to other countries. Life became about having the best job to make the most money that was used to buy everything that came from somewhere else. Without even understanding what they were doing they damaged the fabric of real community while thinking it was all such a huge improvement.

They were told that over-specialization leads to extinction but didn't pay attention to the warning signs. They grew their food in giant mono-culture dirt farms where if one simple thing went wrong the entire crop could be wiped out along with a portion of the population that depended upon harvesting it. They tried to control who was allowed to grow certain things by patenting biological life forms. That paradigm dragged them further into the risk of catastrophic failure. Their business plans ignored the importance of bio-diversity. They thought their farming techniques were technologically advanced, but in reality they were based upon the primitive paradigm of exploitation of both agricultural workers and consumers.

As dirt farmers they used one hundred times the amount of water we use today to produce our crops hydroponically. The underground aquifers were drained to feed their mono-culture crops in the name of profit. They fed antibiotics to their animals and plants alike to compensate for poor husbandry techniques, eventually weakening their own immune systems from eating that food. The development pattern based on the transportation of everything was adopted as the standard of wealthy countries around the world. Eventually there were more people, more cars, bigger highways and more pollution until finally the planet began responding with superstorms and radical climate change.

Usury was legal in those days. All of this mindless growth was financed by a group of people known as the Dominators who charged massive amounts of interest for nearly everything. It was all driven by money created out of nothing as debt. The interest they charged for their printed money put such a burden on the people, the average husband and wife had to work five or six days a week just to keep up with their interest payments. They couldn't conceive of the three day work week we have now. Gramps said that people couldn't really relax. They were always in a hurry to do the next thing. The background tension they lived with was the result of having borrowed money to purchase nearly everything and then having to keep up to pay the interest bill.

The Dominators were arrogant in the extreme and weren't wise enough to honor the vast knowledge of their ancestors. They saw the Earth as something to be subdued and conquered. They were in for a huge surprise. Their global financial system began to collapse from its own weight in 2008. The process took another eleven years. The second great depression was well under way when the kill shot came in 2019.

In those days the people didn't understand the symbiotic relationship that exists between the planets in our solar system and the sun. They didn't understand that all of the planets in our solar system act together in an interconnected electro-magnetic manner to produce the conditions required for biological life here on Earth. In their ignorance they upset the natural balance so badly the ecosystem finally responded in one single moment.

Gramps described the experience, "In 2008 we entered a period of great struggle between common folks everywhere and the few but powerful people who did not want the financial system to change. Over the next seven years discontent grew.

During the years of 2016 and 2017 the battle escalated as the Dominator Agenda began to fail. We were so focused on the repercussions of the meltdown of the worldwide financial system we never made the connection between the collective consciousness of all humans and the reactive state of our entire solar system.

We had been monitoring solar flares for about 20 years so we knew what was possible, we just never thought it would happen to us. When the event finally came we had about one day's notice to prepare. There had been all kinds of warnings before and nothing happened, so some people paid attention, most did not. I was sitting at my desk on the evening of June 12th, 2019 when the kill shot came. It was a coronal mass ejection coming from the sun of a magnitude never before seen in recorded history. All of a sudden the birds stopped singing. There was a crackling sound as if electricity were traveling through the air. It made your hair stand up. The sky lit up and we learned later that the northern lights were seen as far south as Mexico.

I was writing at the time. My computer started smoking and filled my office with that burnt plastic smell. Light bulbs throughout the house exploded and the world went dark as every circuit board in nearly every car, television set, telephone, computer and power station around the world melted. The carnage was fantastic though we didn't see the usual video coverage of it for another year or so because all electronic methods of communication ceased to exist in that moment.

Millions of cars coasted to a halt as the freeways seemed to freeze in place, airplanes fell out of the sky when their engines quit, hospitals went dark. In the year afterward a lot of people died. They had depended upon a distribution system that was no longer able to deliver the goods they required. It was both the end of the old world and the beginning of the new one."

As I read Grandpa's account, I pondered the idea that pretty much everything that had a circuit board stopped moving. They hadn't learned to shield their micro-electronic chips the way we do now. The transportation system came to a halt. The world population had bet their entire civilization on the early days of the micro-chip, without understanding the risks of over-specialization. When the one thing that could destroy all micro-chips happened, they were totally unprepared.

They had created a society where everything came from somewhere else. All of that transportation relied on computer chips to run. When everything stopped moving, they were stuck with only what was left on the shelves where they were. They became painfully aware that their system only had about a five day supply of anything in any particular location. Since they had stopped teaching everyone how to make things and grow food, they found themselves in deep trouble. The interesting thing about the whole experience was that the solar storm didn't kill much biology right away.

Gramps said they felt a little uncomfortable, but people and animals were mostly unaffected. The solar storm just fried their technology. Being deprived of the technology they had placed their trust in, is what killed so many people over the next year.

It's interesting to note that nature caused all the movement to stop in the most non-violent way possible. It took a long time for humanity to understand that Gaia was simply flushing out an irritant that was upsetting her eco-system. During the first year after the solar storm, pollution dropped drastically and the crazy weather patterns evened out. When everything stopped, people had to make do with whatever was around them.

Being an experienced generalist, Gramps and his colleagues had foreseen and talked about what might happen, though it was still a shock when it finally did. They thought collapse would come as a result of the failure of their economic system, not a solar flare. Several years before the event they started a company that produced the first generations of hand powered home food growing machines. These were the primitive ancestors of the personal growing machines we all use to feed ourselves now. That was the beginning of the decentralization movement that literally swept the United States out of necessity.

Up to that time the world wide trend had been toward centralization in every walk of life. Bigger governments were absorbing smaller governments less able to defend themselves. Bigger corporations were taking over the smaller corporations, often by hostile means. Power was being concentrated in fewer and fewer hands. Life had become a struggle between the common man and these giant organizations that viewed the common man only as an account number and payment history.

The trend toward the consolidation of everything was driven by the desire of a very small percentage of powerful people who insisted that they were the ones most qualified to be in control. Overall control of the systems of commerce were being placed in the hands of fewer and fewer people of questionable morality. They didn't see their activities as part of a cycle. They didn't foresee that the pendulum would be swinging back toward massive decentralization in the future. When it started to happen they couldn't cope with the changes.

Before the kill shot on June 12th, self reliance was considered to be a step back in time. No one wanted to grow their own food or make their own clothing or furniture. No one wanted to take the time to learn all the skills for living that we have mastered now. With the gradual collapse of their financial system just before the solar storm, they were surrounded by clues that they had entered a box canyon with no way out, but they didn't see it. They failed to understand the necessity of using their technology in a sustainable way. The local butcher, baker and candlestick maker had been removed from society and replaced by giant retail and manufacturing facilities that all went dark at the same time.

What also went dark was the financial system. When the solar storm fried all the computers, the records of who owed what to whom went up in smoke. All payments ceased. All commerce stopped for a while. The big banks and credit card companies went out of business in the next few months. Gramps said, "Served them right in my opinion." Though nobody openly declared it, all debts simply went unpaid. Here in Montana, no foreclosures were allowed. The people organized a militia to make sure no bank was allowed to come and put anyone out on the street.

He went on to say, "Undeveloped countries that still relied on hand labor to do everything fared much better. They hadn't become used to all of the gadgets that the modern world relied upon. When the big event occurred, their lives didn't really change all that much. Somewhere in their ancient scriptures it said that the meek would inherit the Earth and that is exactly what happened. All of a sudden the entire world wanted to learn what they had always known about living in a close relationship with the land."

Gramps referred to that period as the scariest and happiest time of his life, "When the power went out we realized in short order that nobody was going to come and save us. We had to rely on what we had and the people around us to survive. Once we got over the fear, it was exhilarating. The world didn't have a warehouse of undamaged computer chips that could be delivered to restore our ability to move people and resources. It would be some time before those facilities would be back in service and we could even begin to repair everything.

Immediately we discovered that some older pre-chip vehicles and tractors could be easily repaired. People who owned that equipment were quickly convinced to donate it to the community for the greater good of all. We set up democratic citizen councils to decide what to do with the meager resources we could cobble together. Nobody was allowed an unreasonable profit at the expense of anyone else. Our focus necessarily turned to providing the basic needs of survival for as many people as possible. The great majority of us gave to each other in an unprecedented outpouring of compassion and love."

Gramps goes on, "We understood right away that our priorities were food and warmth. Thank God, the solar storm happened during the summer so we had a little time to prepare for the coming winter. People discovered the hard way that money no longer had much value. If you had something critical to exchange and accepted money for it, you might not be able to use that money to acquire whatever else you might need. Prior to the event, many people thought gold would retain its value in a crisis. Ultimately, that proved not to be the case. You can't eat gold can you? Better to exchange what you had to trade for food, firewood or something that would enhance your survival."

"By a stroke of good fortune some older portable generators managed to survive. They were considered to be objects of the highest value. They were used to get the local machine shops up and running so we could make more hydroponic growing machines and repair as much damaged machinery as we could. Every gas station in town had nearly full tanks, but there were only a few operational cars around. The community council decided that fuel was allowed to be used for generating power, producing food, and bringing in firewood. Across the country, the electrical power grid went off and stayed off for quite a while. The natural gas system went off but was restored much more quickly. In one 24 hour period, everyday reality changed in ways that continued to astound and amaze us for years to come."

"The winter of 2019 was a tough one. The federal government failed and lost control. The Montana State Militia closed the borders so we wouldn't be overrun with refugees. In order to come into our territory you had to prove you had family that lived here before the event. Even so, our population grew. We were far away from the borders and there was no television so we didn't really see much of what happened there.

We lost some friends and neighbors that winter. But the people of our valley came together in a way that was nothing short of miraculous. There was a new purpose evident in our relationships with each other. People that had only been acquaintances became best friends. Those who possessed stored wealth shared freely. Acts of personal heroism occurred on a daily basis. They wouldn't give you the shirt off their back since they needed to stay warm and healthy to serve their families, but they would convince twenty-five people to tear off their pockets and sew you up a shirt of your own.

Up to a point, almost everyone was willing to put their own survival at risk to help those who were less fortunate. The strength that poured forth from our community formed the basis for a new regional culture of mutual concern and cooperation. We talked about how we would return to the old ways of competing for profits once everything was finally restored, but we never did. We liked who we had become and decided to keep on going."

"Strange things happened economically. Before the event people were only willing to pay a dollar and a half for a bar of factory made soap. No individual could make a bar of soap by hand at that price, so traditionally it had to be mass produced to be economical. Very shortly the soap on the store shelves was gone and there was no soap except what we could make for ourselves. All of a sudden a bar of handmade soap was worth a couple dozen eggs and was used judiciously by those who could obtain it. Cottage industries exploded everywhere. Practically every commodity went through a similar shift. Cars, for example, lost their value almost entirely. Chainsaws, hand tools, chocolate and fresh produce were up. Snowmobiles, pleasure boats, skis and art objects were worthless. TV sets had no value at all. Toilet paper was worth a king's ransom. The dawn of each new day required everyone to change how they thought about their world."

"It took 6 years before we started to see the reappearance of devices run by computer chips. Some people wanted to return to the same old patterns of behavior, but the world had already changed. The age of materialism had come to a close. We had discovered that the most valuable thing we all possessed was time. When the old system collapsed we were amazed at how much time we had since we no longer had to pay the interest burden that had become so much a part of our lives in the past. Having the time to live life as a continuous cascade of acts of creativity gave birth to a new standard of wealth.

As our new shielded computers came on line, we used our communication systems to establish direct democracy. We eliminated the middle men and the corruption that used to run our system of government. Now, the people vote directly on every issue. There was an explosion of technology. Every area of endeavor was decentralized from far off locations and brought home. We started to manufacture everything we needed to live comfortably within a hundred miles. Slowly there were meaningful jobs for anyone who wanted to work. Prices for everything became real again. Democracy was established in business. Having a job meant you had a say in how the company you worked for was run. Instead of existing for the benefit of absentee investors, companies now existed for the benefit of everyone who worked there.

We eliminated our dependence on crops grown elsewhere by inventing the processes we use today to grow food at home and particularly to grow food indoors. Our diets changed and became more healthy as a result. The products we created were designed for longevity instead of planned obsolescence. What started out as print on demand in the publishing world became print on demand in the world of parts. Every part for every appliance and artifact we designed was digitally archived. If some part failed, you could place your order with the parts center and they would print it for you that same day on the metal plasma printer or the 3D plastic printer.

Your part would arrive at your home within 24 hours. Making everything repairable, drastically reduced our need to extract resources from nature. It also dramatically reduced the waste stream we had to deal with. We discovered that eliminating waste from every area of our lives translated into more time for everyone.

People didn't travel locally the way they used to. There was no need. The fabric of our communities changed. Local work centers were established so you could walk to work or ride a bike to your job. They were fun places to hang out. Our local work center had small businesses making hydroponic growing machines, soap, candles, leather products, book publishing and sculpture. The next nearest work center made clothing, footwear, pottery and furniture.

Creativity was encouraged in every aspect of our lives and taught to our children. All the kids were raised understanding that they could design what they needed and make it at home. Life was much slower than before. We all took time to live much more deliberately. We took time to enjoy the mountains, the streams and the wildlife. If it snowed heavily we took the day off and went out to play."

"We came together in ways none of us had ever experienced before. During the next decade we developed a new locally oriented worldview based upon love, compassion and forgiveness. A sense of respect and responsibility for one's fellow human beings swept through this valley and touched the hearts of everyone. It was an experience of biblical proportions that influenced everything that happened after that.

An unusual percentage of seers, counselors and healers had made our valley home for decades before the event. Like most of us they were attracted here by the natural beauty. With their guidance we turned within and began to flush out the meanness of the heart that was so much a part of the Dominator culture.

We learned to connect with each other in ways we had never known before. We based our emerging wisdom tradition on making life a celebration of who we had become together. It was a beautiful period. We turned tragedy into peace and happiness on a scale most of us had never known."

Gramps wrote that in 2029. I wanted to share it with you as a little bit of the history that helped create our world, and more importantly who we are in now in 2050. I hope you find inspiration in his words and that you are all well and prospering. Until next time.

Keep Smiling,

Colin Joseph

CHAPTER SIXTEEN

The Letter Translated

I wrote this story to illustrate what might happen if our financial system crumbles for any reason. I'm not asking you to interpret the foregoing story as a prediction of what is going to happen. I'm not trying to predict a coming solar storm though it is quite possible. On September 1st, 1859 the Earth was impacted by the largest and fastest coronal mass ejection ever ex-perienced in recorded history. The plasma wave traveled from the Sun to the Earth at a speed exceeding 5 million miles per hour, covering the 93 million mile distance in only 17 hours. Auroras were seen in the northern hemisphere as far south as the Caribbean. Tele-graph systems all over North America and Europe failed as components that were far more robust than a modern circuit board melted.

We have measured coronal mass ejections of similar magni-tude since 1859 though none have actually impacted our planet. However, we are clearly being shown that the current qualities of collective human consciousness have mutated to such a de-gree that nature is responding to our behavior in ways we have yet to fully understand.

As I write this I am looking out my window and cannot see my beloved mountains that are only 5 miles from where I sit. That's because our valley is full of smoke from wild fires that are currently raging in British Columbia, Idaho and Washington. Here in northwest Montana we see some smoke every year around this time. It's forest fire season here, but the old timers are saying they have never seen it this bad for this long. Our current air quality is on a par with Bejing on a bad day.

That is unheard of in this neck of the woods, which is associated with the pristine natural beauty of Glacier National Park. These conditions appear to be an effect of a prolonged drought being experienced on the west coast for the last few years, which in turn appears to be an effect of global climate change caused by the activities of human beings on this planet. One major component of global climate change is caused by our consumption of fossil fuels in the vehicles we drive, the railroads we run, the airplanes we fly and the ships we move goods in.

With the development of our modern transportation system, a major shift has occurred in the way that we make and distribute the goods we rely on for everyday living. In America and Europe during the 17th, and 18th centuries most consumable goods were produced within a few hundred miles of the people who would buy or trade for them. The butcher, the baker, the chandler, the weaver and the candlestick maker were all in evidence in every town throughout the countryside. The infrastructure for making all of the goods needed to live life was a readily observable part of each community.

Then the captains of the great square rigged sailing vessels of the time discovered that items considered to be common and of little value in one distant location were highly valued at home. Considered to be rare and highly prized in Europe, spices like cinnamon, ginger, pepper, cloves and nutmeg, were so common in India they were considered to have little value and were sometimes used as animal feed. By contrast, items made of metal like swords, cutlery, various kinds of weapons and tools as well as metals in raw form, while common to Europeans, were rare and highly prized in tropical locations.

The captains of the great sailing vessels discovered that they could take a small quantity of European metal goods to far off locations and return with ships brimming with highly prized spices, foods, silks and textiles that brought handsome profits at home. Thus began the modern pre-occupation with accumulating vast profits by always moving everything from here to there.

The trend of chasing profits by exploiting regional differences in the cost of labor has skyrocketed in the last 60 years. During that time period American manufacturers noticed that the cost of cheap third world labor plus the costs of transporting finished goods back to the United States for purchase by consumers, was still substantially less than the cost of manufacturing goods at home. They decided to chase those profits en masse. We are now discovering that the calculations of that cost did not include a value for environmental degradation or lost jobs at home.

While large fortunes have been made by a very small number of people who have successfully taken advantage of this mechanism, major side effects have been imposed upon the American public as a result of that profit taking. There are two very important effects from this trend.

First, we have shipped our manufacturing capabilities overseas creating a shortage of jobs at home. Strangely enough the shortage of jobs at home makes the populace less able to buy the goods that have been produced by cheap labor overseas and shipped back to our shores to be consumed.

Secondly, we have allowed our local manufacturing infrastructure to be sold for scrap. In America you can no longer go down the street and observe how the necessities of everyday life are made. Mostly everything we consume comes from somewhere else. It would take an enormous investment of time and money to restore the capability to meet the needs of the local population with locally produced goods. That doesn't mean it isn't desirable or even mandatory for our survival as a species.

I believe our immediate future contains some serious challenges. In A Letter From The Future, I chose an event apparently caused by nature, that stopped all transportation, to point out how precarious our current position is. If such a thing were to happen, for any reason, would we be able to respond locally in time to avoid the loss of large numbers of humans? We are entering uncharted territory with respect to our collective relationship with nature.

It is becoming clear that the presence of over 7 billion of us is upsetting the ecological balance in ways we have not yet anticipated. The balance isn't upset just because we are here. The balance is upset because of what we have decided to believe is real and the behavior that flows from those beliefs. I fervently hope that eliminating large numbers of people isn't the answer. Learning to live in harmony with the planet and with each other is.

The Dominators have become so engorged on profits that flow from our transportation system and our financial system that if it were all to come to a halt, it appears that millions who do not enjoy those profits would die. I wanted to leave A Letter From The Future with a happy ending. However, we should ask ourselves whether we would really be able to come together in a show of love, compassion and forgiveness for each other under such circumstances. I'm not so sure we would.

While a collapse of our financial system might produce similar results when compared to a natural disaster, the real cause of the tragedy would be rooted in the Dominator Belief System.

One of the blind spots in that system is a lack of perspective known as over-specialization. Our stupidity may be gaining on us.

<u>Extinction Through Over-Specialization:</u> At an annual meeting of the American Association for the Advancement of Science in the early 1950's two research papers were presented. Unbeknownst to each other, two scholars attending the conference presented separate papers, one in biology and one in anthropology. The anthropological paper reviewed the histories of human tribal cultures that had become extinct. The biological paper investigated the histories of biological species that had become extinct.

Each scholar, unaware of the efforts of the other, had come to the same conclusion. They each concluded that the cause of extinction for both biological species and human tribal cultures was a phenomenon called over-specialization. The tribes and species in question had become so specialized in doing things only one way, they lost the ability to adapt to *changing circumstances.* When unforeseen changes occurred, they were unable to react and thus had perished.

In his ground breaking book, Operating Manual for Spaceship Earth, Buckminster Fuller gives the following example of the process of extinction through over-specialization:

"There once was a type of bird that lived on a special variety of micro-marine life. Flying around, these birds gradually discovered that there were certain places in which that particular marine life tended to pocket—in the marshes along certain ocean shores of certain lands. So, instead of flying aimlessly for chance of finding that marine life, they went to where it was concentrated in bayside marshes. After a while, the water began to recede in the marshes, because the Earth's polar ice cap was beginning to increase.

Only the birds with very long beaks could reach deeply enough in the marsh holes to get at the marine life. The unfed short-billed birds died off. This left only the long-beakers. When the bird's inborn drive to reproduce occurred there were only other long-beakers surviving with whom to breed. This concentrated their long-beak genes. So, with continually receding waters and generation to generation inbreeding, longer and longer beaked birds were produced. The waters kept receding, and the beaks of successive generations of the birds grew bigger and bigger.

The long-beakers seemed to be prospering when all at once there was a great fire in the marshes. It was discovered that because their beaks had become so heavy, these birds could no longer fly. They could not escape the flames by flying out of the marsh. Waddling on their legs, they were too slow to escape, and so they perished. This is typical of the way in which extinction occurs—through over-specialization."

Have we generated a modern society in which we have become over-specialized? The answer to that question is absolutely. Our monetary system itself is a form of over-specialization. Our transportation system is a form of over-specialization. We have set up our society so that we must use money to acquire nearly everything we own or consume. We have allowed very small groups of people to control how that money is used and the cost we must pay to use it.

They have consistently demonstrated their willingness and enthusiasm for making non-evolutionary decisions that have a deleterious effect on the rest of humanity in return for short term gratification. The actions of the Dominators are slowly destroying the value of currency on a worldwide basis. What happens if paper money is suddenly perceived to have no value at all? Do we move on to electronic money that has no value or do we create an entirely new system that recognizes what real value is?

Does the profit enhancement enjoyed by a few people, who are in a position to constantly move manufacturing capability from one country to another in pursuit of cheap labor, justify the increased carbon footprint and environmental cost of moving everything around the world all the time? Do the profits enjoyed by the few justify the disruption and destruction of so many lives every time a Dominator decides to withdraw his manufacturing activity from America and move it to China and then move it to Thailand? Do the profits that are flowing to a very few justify the increasing risk that some sort of systemic disruption of the global transportation or monetary system will leave millions of people without the necessities of life? When you add environmental degradation to the risks of over-specialization the answer more and more people are leaning toward is:

No, the benefits enjoyed by the few that are generated by this system do not justify the costs that are being imposed upon the majority of us.

Part of the antidote for over-specialization is to return to making what we consume near our homes. If we re-create a new more high tech version of the butcher, the baker and the candlestick maker at home, we can eliminate a large portion of the environmental cost of transporting goods and chasing profits all over the globe. We can also remove our dependence upon international corporations that are subject to the risks of over-specialization. We can re-establish consumer relationships with local producers who are concerned about what we think of them because we live together. We must regain the ability to afford the cost of our own labor.

Small scale local producers would be much more inclined to listen when their customers declare they do not want to consume GMO products because their success would depend upon the acceptance of that feedback. As it is today, we have little contact with the actual people who make what we consume. The Dominator response to the GMO problem has not been to honor customer wishes, but to bribe congress to pass laws that don't require them to label their products accurately.

In order to re-establish local manufacturing it will be necessary to put quality of life before the illusory rewards of the blind pursuit of profit. We will need to re-acquaint ourselves with the cost of domestic labor and be willing to pay that price. That blow can be softened somewhat by an understanding of what the actual cost for having shipped all our jobs overseas really is. How much the cheap goods at WalMart have really cost is modified by the knowledge that we are buying them because our jobs have been exported overseas and we can't afford anything else.

One of the tasks before us is to completely re-evaluate our monetary system and invent new ways to realize our individual sovereignty as citizens of Earth.

CHAPTER SEVENTEEN

We Hold These Truths
To Be Self Evident

I still believe deeply in certain principles expressed by the founders of the United States of America. I am also aware that all the pontificating in the world is of little value unless it is backed up in thought, word and deed.

I believe it is self evident that creating the highest possible level of freedom for all is commensurate with the intent of creation and the originally stated objectives of the founding fathers of the United States of America.

However, freedom comes with responsibility. We cannot allow a small segment of society to confiscate the freedom of the rest of the people in order to enhance their own. That is not real freedom for all. The attainment of freedom, for the benefit of all, comes with a moral imperative to do unto others only that which you would have done unto you. That is such a simple paradigm, even school kids remember it. It is a way of life that holds honor as one of the highest ideals of human existence. I am saddened to see that so many people, in positions of power, are willing to trade a life of honor for a bigger number on their balance sheet.

Representative Government: The founders of our country intended for there to be a much higher level of democratic participation in deciding how we will run our society. Even though we call ourselves a democracy, business in its entirety is wholly undemocratic. Government of the people, by the people and for the people is the ideal most of us want and the ideal many have given their lives to defend. Yet that ideal has been allowed to be subverted and overpowered by those organizations and special interests that have slowly seized remote control of our government.

I believe it is self evident that the government of the United States no longer represents the will of the people.

Few of us correspond with our elected officials. The government of the United States represents the will of big business, whose armies of lobbyists populate our capital and control the legislative conversation on a daily basis. Unfortunately this state of affairs is now true in all so called democracies that are run by the Dominator Agenda.

Absolute Power Corrupts Absolutely: The fact that power corrupts people has been demonstrated over and over again, not only in the United States but around the world. There are military power structures, political power structures, economic and religious power structures.

I believe it is self evident that the more power is concentrated in any kind of political or economic structure, the more likely that structure will abdicate its original mission and begin to stand only for the preservation and prosperity of those who run it.

The larger a power structure becomes, the less responsive it is to the people it was originally designed to serve and the more responsive it becomes to those who benefit from its favors. If that is human nature, it should be a part of human nature we need to organize ourselves to overcome.

We keep trying to reform one large power structure after another only to discover that we are surrounded by systemic corruption on all fronts. The big banks fleece their investors, well known car makers cheat on emission standards, the Federal Reserve inflates our currency while serving the interests of Wall Street, scandal after scandal plagues our political system and on and on. I'm not an anarchist but we must find ways to change our system. We must find a way to re-introduce a sense of honor and responsibility into our culture.

I believe it is self evident that we need to reduce the size of all power structures that are capable of causing systemic economic harm to millions if not billions of people.

Any organization that is too big to fail because its failure will cause the destruction of our financial system is very simply just too big and should be broken up into much smaller entities.

Even though our financial system is corrupt, it would be more desirable for all if we didn't destroy it, but caused it to change for the better gradually.

While we were all occupied making more money to pay the constantly inflating debt service on goods that were already in our possession, the gradual degradation of the American Dream took place. We became so engrossed in the trappings of financed materialism we didn't even notice that the very fabric of a free society was being eroded around us.

Reversing the process by placing the interests of the many above the interests of the few is directly contrary to the way the modern world is built. Such a mega-change in our operating system will bring howls of protest from the political and economic elite. Such a mega-change in our operating system implies a vast restructuring of national affairs. In particular, it calls for a complete restructuring of our monetary system. In order for freedom to take its place as the central theme behind our operating system we will need to re-establish the power of self determination and self governance at the local level.

Part of the reason both communism and socialism have failed to deliver the quality of life they promised, is because they demand a central concentration of power, a ruling class that is capable of enforcing the mandatory redistribution of assets and wealth from afar.

We simply do not trust the motives of those in control of such power. Central planning does not work. We really don't like it when bureaucrats in some far off city, who have placed themselves above the laws we must obey, make a decision that makes our lives harder than they were before.

Central planning is not responsive to the wide range of conditions found in the different regions of our country. The people in Washington have quite different concerns than the people in Montana. For that matter, the people who live in cities have quite different concerns than the people who live in the rural countryside. One size does not fit all. Power concentrated in fewer and fewer hands is not responsive to the needs of the people.

As Americans we whole heartedly object to a society in which anyone in government is capable of demanding and enforcing the mandatory redistribution of assets and wealth from afar. Yet, that is exactly what we have created.

The difference in the American experiment is that the power to cause such a redistribution is in the hands of the private sector organizations that rule our government. During 2007 and 2008 Wall Street aided by the Federal Reserve caused a systemic redistribution of assets and wealth from the hands of the American population directly into the bank accounts of the largest financial institutions in the land.

Many millions of hard working American families were robbed of their life savings. That redistribution has not stopped. That redistribution is so large in scope it effects the monetary systems of countries around the world. How is that different from the redistribution of wealth and assets from the people to the state? In both cases the fruits of the labor of common people are stripped away by forces that are beyond their control. We have to find a way to reverse that trend.

Income Inequality is natural, it is very like bio-diversity. Enforced economic equality has never worked and never will. One reason enforced economic equality has never worked is because the people in charge of implementing it band together and create a privileged class of enforcers thus negating the very premise for which they stand. Another reason enforced economic equality has never worked is that, no matter what laws you make, you cannot remove self interest from the human equation.

Individuals should have the right to prosper at different rates according to their ability to create positive outcomes <u>for the benefit</u> of society. Those who achieve on behalf of society have earned the right to prosper and should be celebrated for their contribution. Those who are capable of achieving on behalf of society, but choose instead, to prey upon society should have their means reduced by the society they have betrayed.

Income inequality is not a bad thing so long as it remains in balance. It is no longer in balance around the world. Why does one person need hundreds of millions of times more than is required to live comfortably? The only reason people want that is to accumulate the power to subjugate other people and control world events for their own personal aggrandizement.

When a small number of people control the rest of the population, then society at large is subjected to the morality that was used to acquire that level of control. The current dismal state of human affairs in 2016 is the direct product of being subjected to the morality of the minority who are in control.

CHAPTER EIGHTEEN

Globalism
and the
New World Order

Globalism is the process whereby the disparate belief systems of the people of the world gradually merge into one. Whether we like it or not this process is under way. It is being accelerated on a daily basis by all forms of media and especially by the internet. Great danger lurks within this relatively new phenomenon and great hope as well.

An epic battle is under way to convince humanity that the best hope for a thriving future lies in the world of materialism. The belief system that has grown up around materialism promotes the idea that the people who have acquired the most material wealth are the happiest among us and should naturally be held in great esteem by the rest of humanity.

By definition, the term economic exclusivity means that the real value derived from material wealth requires a separation between those who are exclusive and those who are not. The

more exclusive, the wider the gap between the haves and the
have-nots.

*The idea that economic exclusivity is desirable implies that
we are all in competition for access to the resources we need to
live and it is reasonable for there to be a wide gap between the
winners and the losers in the worldwide competition.*

Looking at life like it is a competition for who gets the most
of everything automatically creates a distinction between the
winners and losers. The winners are entitled to the lion's share of
everything, not because they are the wisest or the most creative,
but because they command the power of capital and are clever
enough to make it happen. The rest of us are apparently here to
serve the winners.

That is being demonstrated on a daily basis in all aspects of
our economic lives. Television shows the anointed riding in
their limousines and flying in their jets and suggests that we all
should want to be them. Strangely enough and contrary to our
cultural myths, they are rarely portrayed in the stories we tell as
being happy.

The relatively new phenomenon of universal interconnectivity represented by the Internet and the system of communications
satellites that now surround the planet is exposing us to each
other at a level never before experienced in history. The danger
level of the new phenomenon of interconnectivity rises when it
is used to proliferate the Dominator Agenda as the truth we
should all subscribe to.

The old school is still teaching that the mission of life is to
achieve supremacy, in any way possible, over whatever you see
that impedes your ability to make more money. The old school
still wants to promote the paradigm that economic exclusivity is

good. Economic exclusivity is what distinguishes the truly deserving from everyone else.

In my experience, more and more people are becoming dissatisfied with the concept that exclusivity is good for humans. More and more ordinary people in the United States are aware that our political leadership and our business leadership, clearly see themselves as a class above we the people. The general population believes that those in power are corrupt, inept and possibly even treasonous to the objectives this country was founded upon. To quote the Oxfam report one more time:

"This massive concentration of economic resources in the hands of a few people represents a significant threat to inclusive political and economic systems. Instead of moving forward together, people are increasingly separated by economic and political power, inevitably heightening social tensions and increasing the risk of societal breakdown."

The Dominator Agenda has become so powerful in the United States that during the three years between 2009 and 2012— 95% of all income gains went to the top 1% of the population with only 5% of income gains to be distributed amongst the remaining 95% of the population.[7] A pretty dismal statistic considering that real inflation is still erasing even those meager gains in the purchasing power of 95% of the population.

Despite our government's claims to the contrary, everyone with a household budget knows that their money does not go as far today as it did one year ago. Average citizens are becoming suspicious that there is a relationship between consolidation of power at the top economic echelons of society and their fears that the future will not be as bright as the past.

The New World Order: The economic forces that are shaping world affairs are currently engaged in an unprecedented process of consolidation. Mergers and acquisitions are driven by the enormous fees and insider trading windfalls collected by investment banks and shareholders every time a multi-billion dollar deal closes. Corporations are bringing inordinate amounts of pressure to bear on our law makers to ensure this process continues. Consolidation is taking place in every area of commercial endeavor creating bigger and bigger multi-national conglomerates. Since Lehman Brothers failed in September of 2008, $11 trillion dollars in mergers and acquisitions have been done or await completion.[8]

Every time Company A merges with Company B there is a duplication of staff not only in the management structure, but also in the labor force and in the supply chain. The pink slips begin to flow as the holy pursuit of bean counter efficiency is applied, resulting in increased revenues for investors. Thousands lose their jobs as the investor class consolidates their power and walks away with more and more profit.

The very foundations of a vibrant society are being laid to waste. The big fish are gobbling up the smaller fish using the zero interest rate central bank printed money known as Quantitative Easing.[9] Under our current system, we, the people, are losing a greater and greater percentage of living wage jobs, and will ultimately pay the costs of that printed money which is funding obscene profit taking for Wall Street gamblers.

Every time Company A merges with Company B the choices that distinguished the product lines provided by the two companies start to disappear as well. Company A had 5 kinds of pickles on its shelves and Company B had 5 other kinds of pickles on its shelves. The bean counters, who have studied such things, have determined that anything more than 6 kinds of pickles is a needless duplication. So, after the merger, four kinds of pickles disappear and the supply chain companies that made them are sent back into the "free market" in a race to find new retail relationships before their income losses prove to be fatal.

No thought is given to what happens to the people who depended upon those companies for their livelihoods. The more things are standardized the less choice there is. The more one size fits all, the less diversity there is across the board. The less general diversity there is, the more humanity is in danger of being damaged by artificially induced shortages of goods and services.

The foregoing depiction of the consolidation of power in fewer and fewer hands is what is euphemistically referred to as:

The New World Order

In my view the end game of the New World Order is to eventually bust one national currency system after another in an orgy of profit taking and then in the midst of total chaos, put a new one world electronic currency in place, thus finally consolidating global control in the hands of "the winners."

When that finally happens, no exchange of goods or services will be allowed to take place without being monetized and recorded so it can be properly taxed. The people will have no voice in what those tax rates are. Everything you ever do economically will be recorded in a data base along with your electronic identity. The New World Order will have direct access to your bank accounts and will be allowed to deduct tax payments directly from you. When the consolidation of power in the hands of the few reaches its apogee, the subjugation of humanity by the New World Order will finally be complete.

"Give me control of a nations currency and I care not who makes its laws." Baron Mayer Amschel Rothschild

Who is the State? The processes that run big business are not democratic! The processes that run big business are wholly dictatorial. As an employee of Company A or Company B, the average worker has no say in the ultimate direction either company takes. In the United States we created unions to battle this trend. Then we watched helplessly as our unions were taken over by criminals and Dominators and their mission subverted.

The politicians we elected to inhabit the chambers where our laws are made, are busy running a special favors mill pandering to the interests of Wall Street and big business. Our elected politicians are actually helping Wall Street and big business redistribute as much wealth as possible from the common people to the wealthiest class as fast as it can be accomplished.

That is why the Oxfam Report says what it says.

For the most part, our politicians and business leaders do not consult with working people to discover what wisdom might lurk there. Working people are considered to have no wisdom to contribute and have been shut out of the legislative process in the United States. Thus, the people have not participated in the policy decisions allowing the Fed to print a record amount of money and use it to fuel a mergers and acquisitions frenzy on Wall Street. Mark my words, the people will pay the cost for that speculation to the tune of trillions of dollars.

The number of economic relationships you have with organizations, to whom you are nothing but an account number and source of revenue, is increasing. At the same time the number of economic relationships you have with principals who own the businesses you buy from and who live in your neighborhood is shrinking to the point of extinction. The process of consolidation I am referring to continually places a smaller and smaller percentage of the world population in political and financial control of everyone else.

The purpose of the consolidation of power in fewer and fewer hands is not to liberate you or to enhance your freedom.

Central banks all over the world are printing money as fast as they can to fund the consolidation process. The more consolidation that is financed by money created from nothing, the less jobs there are and the more all currencies inflate. As the money in the possession of common people dwindles in value, the less goods and services they are able to buy. As fewer and fewer goods are bought, the more consolidation must occur to trim the fat from labor and management in order to maintain investment returns. After all, nothing is more important than return on investment. Slowly we spiral down into worldwide recession. If this process is allowed to continue we will spiral down into worldwide depression.

It is hard to say exactly how the New World Order will finally manifest. I don't think anybody can really know that. However, we can intuit what it might be like to live in such a world. In any country you can name, the people who are in control of the currency of each national system are the people who set policy for everything else that occurs. Capital is now in control. We are witnessing a takeover of government wherein privately held big business has become the state.

In China today, the state is in control of business, therefore the state is big business. In Russia, the oligarchs are in control of business and the oligarchs are now the state, therefore the state is big business. In the United States big business now runs and has essentially become, the state.

Big business now occupies the unelected chamber of the United States Government that sits above the house and senate and dictates what they do. It even writes the laws, and the talking points in favor of those laws, and delivers them directly to the political class. Through the Federal Reserve, and its highly successful skills at market rigging, Wall Street is in control of U.S. economic policy. The Federal Reserve is a privately held corporation staffed with people who are loyal to the interests of big business. Most of the people who control U.S. economic policy have proven they are not loyal to the common people but only to their own privileged class.

The United States of America was founded upon the principle of no taxation without the direct representation of the will of the people in the legislative process. The people are supposed to have a voice in how the costs of our economy are distributed. That is no longer the case. The people are now subjected to the whims of a business/state that is capable of effecting the economic and social lives of hundreds of millions of people in a negative way, without their prior knowledge or permission.

Our only recourse is to vote out the old politicians and vote in the new ones who essentially stand for the same values having risen through the ranks of our political farm team system. The state should be run by real statesmen and stateswomen who have dedicated their lives to the well being of the people and whom are willing to sacrifice a small portion of their careers to serve that ideal.

Our elected officials should swear an oath to eliminate debt and servitude in any way possible and to champion the cause of increased freedom and prosperity for common folks everywhere. How could that possibly be bad for the people at the top of our economic system? How could that be bad for the economy?

The founders of our great country intended that the government of the United States of America dedicate itself to being the protector of the people. Our government was supposed to protect and defend the people against all enemies both foreign and domestic. Our real enemies are those people who are willing to use their power to conscript the population and severely limit access to the real freedom and liberty we have given so many of our lives to defend over the last 240 years. The point that such a conscription has already taken place will hit home, with more power than ever before, when the next recession which is caused by the Dominators and is now coming to a boil, arrives in your neighborhood.

The state has become big business. Big business has become the state. The very real problem is that big business does not stand for the ideals of freedom and liberty we have always cherished as the founding principles of the United States.

I want to open up a deep inquiry into what is best for humanity to larger and larger numbers of people. I believe the directions we decide to take in the future should be the result of the inclusion of the will of as many people as possible. I hope to demonstrate that we are all, by nature, in a position to effect positive evolutionary change for the benefit of humanity as a whole.

A critical part of our ability to step into the role of agents for positive change is for each of us to decide what we stand for and what we believe in.

The process of globalism is happening whether we like it or not. The energy behind that process is manifesting a world culture that is the result of those beliefs. If we don't like the way the world is unfolding then it would be wise to re-examine our belief systems. We are finally coming to the realization that the illusion of economic exclusivity actually retards material progress for most of humanity by confiscating it for its own benefit.

A deep look at the natural world reveals that bio-diversity is a fundamental ingredient within all sustainable organic systems. The concept of bio-mimicry is gaining acceptance around the world. Bio-mimicry is based upon the idea that nature has already solved the problems of the sustainability of biological systems in ways that human beings would do well to emulate in world affairs.

We have demonstrated beyond a shadow of doubt that eliminating diversity in any biological system increases the probability that extinction through over specialization could occur. We would do better if we recognized that this principle applies to humanity as the temporarily dominant biological system on our planet. We would build a stronger future for all if we understood that the decentralization of power is healthy for human beings. Dare we look so far into the future as to embrace the possibility that what we really want is individual and universal self government according to a sustainable moral code?

The bigger any power structure is, the harder it falls, and the more damage it does when it falls.

Despite the presence of this wisdom, world leaders still seem to be committed to placing more and more power in fewer and fewer hands, thus eliminating diversity of belief and behavior in all power structures and resulting in a New World Order of subjugation.

The New World Order places the interests of the few above the interests of the many. That is the paradigm upon which the modern world is built.

CHAPTER NINETEEN

Waking From Jefferson's Nightmare

Forty-seven years after the first picture of our blue planet was taken from space, we are just beginning to realize that humanity is a single species inhabiting a fragile spaceship with limited resources on board. Prior to the modern era, we thought the world was so big, there would always be more room to move on once we defiled the camping spot we were living in.

That's no longer true. The giant world we have lived on for so long is becoming smaller and smaller as we analyze and catalog every square foot of it. The exponential growth of the human population is approaching its apogee indicating that perhaps there are other systems coming to their logical conclusion at the same time.

The fractional reserve monetary system demonstrated its interdependence in 2007 as the collapse of American real estate values caused similar collapses to ripple through the worldwide financial system. After decades of clues, we are just beginning to be aware that what we choose to do locally, now effects everyone globally. Though the knowledge is ancient, we are finally discovering the extent to which all human beings are connected.

We have had World Wars before but never a Global Financial Crisis! The fact that the financial crisis is global and that it is still going on 8 years later, puts special emphasis on the understanding that there is something really wrong with the system that runs the world. Like all Ponzi schemes, Fractional Reserve Banking relies on continued growth in order to exist. When any condition surfaces that prevents that growth from continuing, the system collapses and you pay the bill.

History shows us that some Ponzi schemes collapse gradually, others collapse immediately and violently. So far this one is collapsing gradually. So far, most Americans still have food on the table and gas in the car. The Federal Reserve has been running the printing presses "red hot" in an effort to stave off the inevitable conclusion. That is very like trying to put out the fire by pouring gasoline on it. At some point in the not too distant future, the inflationary cycle will peak again.

"Anyone that believes exponential growth can go on forever in a finite world is either a madman or an economist."
Kenneth Boulding Economist.

Fractional Reserve Banking has been the engine that stimulated the amazing growth in the production of material goods that we have experienced over the last 60 years. We all thought we were witnessing the American Dream in operation. However, we are now discovering that those growth rates were accomplished in large part by borrowing from the future and not by some inherent miracle hidden within the vaults of Capitalism. What that really means is, all that growth was not genuine.

Like a thief in the night, the Fractional Reserve Banking system, along with the rampant speculation it always encourages, has left, not only the American public, but also our nation mired within Jefferson's Nightmare. That nightmare is taking the form of an enormous debt burden that hangs over our heads resulting in the potential loss of our property, just the way Jefferson said it would. That debt burden now threatens to destroy everything we have worked so hard to build over the last 240 years.

I want to be crystal clear that the reason we have such an enormous debt burden is not because we have borrowed an extraordinary amount of money from some mystery country.

The reason we have such an enormous debt burden is because we have allowed a highly privileged class of politicians, bankers and Wall Street speculators to walk away with the value of our money and leave us holding a bag of debt in return.

This process has been growing up around us since the days of the American Revolution. It came over from Europe on the boat with the pilgrims. It has infiltrated every market and caused the mutation of all prices along with the steady inflation of our currency, until a dollar in Jefferson's day is worth only 4 cents today.

That value has not simply ceased to exist. The secret money system has allowed the Dominators of the Aristocracy of Capital to confiscate that value and hoard it in their vaults and bank accounts. They have also wasted a great deal of it. That is why income inequality is so pronounced in today's world. We have not only allowed these people to throw the population into debt slavery, but we are individually paying the cost of being kept in debt slavery as well. To make matters somewhat worse, the people of the United States and of the world, who have been subjected to this system, still do not understand what has happened to them.

Baron Rothschild hit the nail on the head when he said there will be no opposition from the few who are interested in the system's profits or dependent upon its favors. Even today, in the face of the knowledge contained in this book, there are those for whom the system has worked. Why should they be concerned? In their experience, the Dominator Agenda has served them well. They should be concerned, because the Baron's secret money system is on the road to destruction by its own hand.

Baron Rothschild also said that the great body of people who can't understand the tremendous advantage capital gets from operating the system will bear its burden without complaint. However, the people of the world are beginning to understand and are starting to complain. For everyone that is secure in the favors of the Dominator Agenda, there are many more who are experiencing the **terminal fatigue** that sets in from decades of trying to outrun the loss of value in their lives.

Despite the distaste I have developed for the secret money system, I maintain that it would be better for all if we did not sit by and allow it to collapse. It would be better for all if we caused one aspect of it to change at a time in an effort to avoid total chaos. In order to do that we will have to take the immediate and painful steps required to change it into something that neither subjugates the population nor requires infinite growth in order to exist. In order to discuss those changes we will need to create some definitions:

What is Speculation? For the objectives of this chapter I'll define speculation as the process of buying low, rigging markets, and selling high for the purpose of acquiring wealth without actually creating anything of real value on behalf of society.

What is Real Value? Real value appears when we combine labor, creativity and raw materials to produce goods that society can use to extend the number of forward days it can exist.

Based upon the foregoing definitions, here are a few suggestions as to what changes would be appropriate for us to make in order to wake from Jefferson's Nightmare. Many more will be needed:

1. Curtail Speculation: I have not made an exhaustive study of the process of speculation. I don't want to become a mindless puritan preaching from the pulpit that all speculation is bad. It is possible that some speculation performs a useful balancing function within a healthy economy. However, it shouldn't be difficult to understand that the rampant extraction of real value from a finite system of resources by too many people, who don't create real value, causes a shortage of both goods and cash. That is what we call a recession, or worse, a depression.

Speculation is attractive because it allows people to amass great wealth without doing much to earn it. That is to say, without creating anything of real value in return. That is the crux of the matter. When the number of people making a fortune without creating value gets out of balance with the number of people who do create real value, the results are what we see around us—Extreme income inequality and a widening financial gap between working people and successful speculators, accompanied by high unemployment.

In the Capitalist value system, any amount of money one can make without going to jail is considered fair game and morally acceptable. The Global Financial Crisis is the direct result of that belief system.

We must find a way to curtail speculation. One of the worst examples of the state of collective human consciousness is our willingness to enslave others so we can take a free ride. The equivalent system in the natural world is parasites. We have allowed the speculators to take over the financial world. Sure, speculators work hard at it, but it's neither an honorable nor a regenerative profession.

We need to agree on a way to measure the damage caused by too much speculation. Then we need to take steps to curtail it. If you are handling a giant merger or acquisition, you should be required to demonstrate the real value and the number of new jobs that society will derive from the transaction. If you cannot make that demonstration, the transaction should be refused. If you profit by rigging a market, without creating real value, you should pay a punitive tax or fine for having done so.

2. Sever the Connection: We must find a way to sever the connection between those who participate in creating monetary policy and those who profit from it. We didn't give the fox the keys to the hen house. By carefully observing the machinations of society, the fox taught himself how to make keys. The only ones who needed to know, were the ones the fox enlisted to help carry away the chickens.

Those who create monetary policy cannot be allowed to profit from it.

Those who are expert at creating monetary policy should be paid a reasonable wage for their expertise and serve at the pleasure of the population they support. We must learn that the prosperity of the population as a whole is more important to the survival of humanity than the extreme prosperity of any single individual.

3. Raise the Fractional Reserve Rate: Naturally, the truth is more complicated, but the basic fractional reserve rate in the United States is roughly 10 percent. The secret money system is so pervasive that our entire economy has become dependent upon the creation of money as debt. The parallel to drug addiction is exact. Our addiction to borrowing money created from nothing as debt is what appears to allow us to have the things we want in life, yet it is the very thing that is destroying us from within. The Federal Reserve's only solution is to print money like there is no tomorrow, which there may not be if they keep it up.

We need to begin to wean ourselves from fractional reserve drugs by raising the percentage of reserves that a bank must hold, perhaps as high as 80 percent and maybe higher. Reducing the fractional reserve rate is the quickest way to slow the creation of money as debt. Reducing the worldwide rate that artificial money is created as debt is our highest priority. This should be done carefully and gradually but also immediately.

4. Make Money Lending a Public Utility: We have let the same people who create disastrous monetary policy walk away with the real value of our currency as a result of creating that monetary policy. They are so dependent upon the favors of this system they have become blind to the damage they are doing.

Society allows a small group to profit from the use of our currency systems while leaving society with the expenses caused by that use. No business man would condone such a plan as being fair, unless of course, he was on the receiving end of the con. In the face of that opportunity, morality no longer appears to be a factor. That needs to change.

Since society pays the cost of operating the currency system, that system rightfully belongs to the people. It is the people's money supply. The business of creating money from nothing as debt should become a non-profit enterprise. The first step in that process would be to audit the Federal Reserve. The practice of charging confiscatory interest rates on home mortgages and credit cards should also stop.

Except for the wages we pay to those who have service jobs in the banking industry, all profits from the activity of creating money as credit or debt should be returned to the people or used to otherwise drastically reduce the cost of borrowed money. The elimination of the interest burden you have been paying for years would be a significant improvement in your household budget.

It will take smarter people than I to engineer how that works. It's important that we get the principles right. We should be concentrating on increasing the overall prosperity of working people to the point where living on borrowed money is no longer a requirement. Those who currently make their living from interest will have to adjust, just as the rest of us that depended upon the fraudulent system of Fractional Reserve Banking have had to adjust while it fails.

5. Stop Paying the Vig: The Vig is a street term referring to a confiscatory interest rate charged by a loan shark, that is so high it enslaves the borrower and prevents them from ever being able to reduce the balance due on the loan. The Vig allows the loan shark to "own" his victims.

The old fashioned version of the American Dream is the one where the vitality of the American economy allowed ordinary citizens to work hard and save enough money to open a small business. They were able to buy the tools and materials required to open for business with cash. That business model was based upon the equity of savings, meaning that the small business person would own the assets of his or her business free and clear.

Decades ago, the American people understood that such a dream was possible if one was capable of running faster than one's household bills, so the required investment could be saved. Ordinary people knew they would have a much better chance of being successful if they had no business debts.

During the 1950's and 60's our economy gradually shifted from an equity economy to a debt based economy. That shift was caused by an increase in the creation of money from nothing as debt. The Aristocracy of Capital realized there was a vast untapped market in retail credit creation. As more and more money was created from nothing in the form of debt, the currency began to lose value at a higher and higher rate.

It became much more difficult to start a small business with savings. It became necessary for grass roots business people to finance the creation of their small businesses. Where it was once unthinkable to borrow money to start such a venture, now every small business budget contains a line item for the debt service on money borrowed to establish the business. Rather than owning their own business, most people went looking for a job.

Thus, we sent a message to the Dominators— If we can have what we want now, we are willing to bet we can pay the Vig in the future. That turned out to be a bad bet. Over time, the process of creating money from nothing devalued our currency to the point where new generations had no memory of saving up to do anything. The U.S. savings rate is now at 5%. The reason it's so low is because the Vig is growing. The more the Vig grows, the less people are able to do anything besides pay the Vig. The more we pay the Vig with borrowed money, the more the Vig grows.

The Vig is now a major component in the price of everything. The people who mine the raw materials to make things have financed their growth with fake money. The people who make the machines used to manufacture goods from raw materials have financed their growth with fake money. Every step of the processes used to bring your food, clothing and household goods to market is financed with money created from nothing upon which the Vig is owed.

The Vig is growing so large it is becoming the biggest cost included in the price of everything. I have outlined how the Vig equals as much as 80% of the cost you pay to own your home. The Vig is taking over household budgets and national budgets.

Practically every nation on earth is deeply concerned about the growing percentage of their gross domestic product that is required just to pay the Vig on their national debt. We are beginning to see that we have all been imprisoned by the loan sharks of the world. We are beginning to watch Jefferson's Nightmare unfold right before our eyes.

We have arrived in the clutches of a global financial crisis because the Dominators chose to make a business out of loaning money created from nothing. The economic troubles that are so prevalent around the world are the result of this subterfuge. The solution now being played out by Wall Street, our government and the Federal Reserve is to print more money created from nothing at a faster rate than ever before. You don't need to be a genius to figure out where that will take us.

What would life be like if there were no Vig? The amount of money you need to live would be cut in half. Prices would return to honest levels. Families would once again prosper. You would no longer face the prospect of periodically losing everything you worked your life away to earn. Boom and bust cycles would disappear. The people who made it their life's work to defraud you would go out of business. Boo Hoo. Justice isn't always gentle. Maybe someday soon we will all get together and decide to stop paying the Vig at the same time.

6. Forgive Unfair Debt: Since debt is growing exponentially when compared to the production of real value, some form of debt forgiveness is going to need to be applied on a macro scale. The holders of debt will scream foul. After all, they maneuvered us into debt fair and square. How do we decide who is allowed to collect their debts and who must forgive? Again it is important that we get the principles right. According to what criteria should anyone be able to demand that another forgive the debt he is owed?

Between 1991 and 2007 the big banks in the United States revved up the credit machine and caused enormous inflation in housing prices. They made hundreds of billions of dollars by loaning money created from nothing. Then, in their zeal to keep making those profits they inflated our currency to the point of collapse.

The recession of 2007 & 2008 was the nastiest since the great depression of 1929. The people who loaned you the money to buy your home, and who profited from it, were the same people who caused you to lose your job and the same people who subsequently foreclosed upon you and took not only your home but your life savings along with it. If you are not mad about that you should be, whether it happened to you or not.

Those people and institutions should have been forced to forgive your debt. They should have rightfully been forced to absorb the loss. The government of the United States sued the big banks for mortgage fraud. Led by Bank of America, JP Morgan Chase, Citi-group and Wells Fargo, 20 of the largest banks in the world have been fined over 235 billion dollars for mortgage fraud. That's just a fraction of the amount they walked away with. No one went to jail. Very little of that money ever made its way back to the people who were damaged.

I believe in the right to personal property for ordinary citizens. But, when the right to personal property of a large corporation allows it to commit crimes against humanity, then that corporation should be forced to forgive the debts it has created and forfeit their claim on the property that secured that debt. One way to change that culture is to make senior executives legally liable for such systemic crimes. Then we will see changes.

7. Clean Up the Government: Jefferson clearly described a government of the people, by the people and for the people. In the Declaration of Independence he wrote that the power of government is derived from the consent of the governed. In 2015 only 14 percent of the people approved of the job congress is doing. The only contact members of congress seem to have with the general population is through rigged opinion polls.

Go to Washington and call your senator's office. Tell them that you are a concerned citizen and would like an appointment with your senator to discuss the issues of the day. See if that appointment is granted. If you do not represent some organization of constituents or some large corporation, it is very likely your voice will not be heard much less acted upon. We haven't had government for the people for a long time. What we do have is government of the corporations, by the corporations and for the corporations.

There are many more changes that should be considered. By now you must think there are armies of villains who have you in their cross hairs and are waiting to pull the trigger. There are. I want you to be riled up. If we don't take the actions that will be necessary to wake from Jefferson's Nightmare soon, there may dire consequences for all of us.

The practice of creating money from nothing depicted in the pages of Jefferson's Nightmare is the most important political issue of our time. It is the root cause of our troubles with unemployment, price inflation, entitlements, crime and even war. Allowing a very small percentage of the global population to steal from everyone else, by creating money from nothing, is a crime against humanity. Yet, it's not even being discussed in our political debates. It's time to wake up!

CHAPTER TWENTY

The American Spirit

When I say that I am proud to be an American, I have to think deeply about what that means to me. I grew up in a small mid-western Ohio town on the shores of Lake Erie. As a kid, I never thought much about what it might be like to live anywhere else. I was too busy just being a kid. One of the things I did notice was that the topography of northern Ohio rarely presents one with an opportunity to see anything that is more than a few miles away. I majored in design at a southern Ohio college. The late 60's were a time of great cultural upheaval. I wanted to create something new. When I was 21 years old I made a break for it and came out west. I landed in the high desert of Taos, New Mexico where the adventures began.

During the winter of 1971, I fell in love with the pink, purple and deep red sunsets reflected off of the Sangre De Cristo range of the Rocky Mountains. I remember declaring that I wanted to get down to the very most basic way of life, to rub my nose in the dirt of mother earth, to see what it took to live simply in a deep relationship with the land. I thought the experience would make me a better person. I think it did. Over the next few years, my young wife and I lived in a succession of tents and small cabins. We migrated to the North Fork Valley of the Gunnison River in Colorado where I fell in love with the West Elk mountain range. In 1972, my wife and I delivered our lovely baby daughter in a tipi during a snow storm. In 1973, I borrowed a two year old, green-broke Morgan mare named Bonnie Blaze so I could take a job as a ditch rider.

Every day I would saddle Bonnie Blaze and load my mule with shovels and traps. My job was to ride the ditch trail five miles up Mount Gunnison and five miles back, trapping beaver to make sure the snow melt that came off the mountain continued to flow down the irrigation ditch to the fruit farmers in the valley below. The wonderful thing I discovered about horse travel is that I was able to see and feel the mountain landscape at 2 miles an hour while my horse did all the work. I rode through the pine forests and the aspen forests and broke out just south of Snowshoe Mesa where I could see for a hundred miles.

Every day I'd tie off the ponies and just sit on a rock trying to feel the depth of the big space around me and my place in it. Slowly, I began to understand that the ability to see far is a multi-dimensional experience. Somehow it filled a void in my soul. I have never wanted to live where I couldn't see far, ever again.

Both a spiritual quest and the pressures of parenthood led us to Encinitas California in '76 where once again we delivered another child at home. My need to see far wasn't really satisfied by looking out over the ocean. Now, I understand that's simply because I'm a mountain person. I began a career as a Southern California home builder with the enthusiasm of youth. After 16 years of marriage I was made aware that the mother of my children and the love of my life were not going to be the same person.

I was already going through the divorce when she appeared. One of our first dates was to climb Mount Shasta together. We discovered that we both had an inner need to see far and to be in the mountains. I proposed to her in a pup tent at Crag Lake in the Desolation Wilderness of the High Sierras. 2016 is our thirtieth year together.

In 1996 we found ourselves back in Colorado. For the next 12 years we rode the Flattops Wilderness together, she, on a rock solid gelding named Semper Fi, which means always faithful. I rode my dearly loved paint mare, China Dancer, a snorty and somewhat frilly creature of rare and unusual beauty. We spent those years riding above 10,000 feet, through some of the most pristine alpine wilderness on the planet.

On the back of a napkin I calculated that we must have ridden the equivalent of coast to coast across the United States during that time, always through magnificent spaces where we could see really far. We both felt the presence of the American Spirit in that landscape, the spirit that drove our pioneers to explore the west. That spirit became a part of us and lives within us still. We managed to outlive our horses and miss them terribly. Our memories of riding together are some of the most precious we have. But, life goes on.

One thing led to another and now we live in northwest Montana. I'm deeply in love with my wife, the Swan Mountains and Glacier Park. This is called the Big Sky Country for good reason. Part of being in a place where you can see far, is that the sky is as much a feature as the land or the mountains. The big sky is a source of constant amazement. It's all about the clouds. They are never the same, they are always new, always finding a fresh way to reflect the light. They are inspired. They part on a clear night to reveal the full moon, the stars and the wonder of the milky way.

These days, my wife and I enjoy the reflections of the big sky on the high mountain lakes and rivers we explore by kayak. I am completely addicted to being here. More than that, I need the big sky just to stay sane.

I have lived in Ohio, New Mexico, Colorado, California, Idaho and Montana. I have chopped wood and carried water to live. I've sat in unheated outhouses praying for fast results while a mid-winter blizzard howled outside. I've bathed in a tin tub with water heated on the wood stove. I know what it means to live in deep relationship with the land. I've spent a considerable amount of time sitting quietly on the edge of a 2,000 ft deep canyon in nature's silence, watching carefully as the river below twinkled in the sunlight and the bald eagles soared overhead. I particularly like the bald eagles. It is no mistake that they symbolize the freedom of the American Spirit.

Through all of those experiences and many more, I've come to have a deep respect for the American People who inhabit our most remote places. For the most part, they are the kindest, most generous people you could ever hope to meet. There is no one I'd rather have at my back in a crisis. I love the American West, but I've been around long enough to know that all of our sacred land from coast to coast reflects different aspects of the great beauty of mother nature. America is a sacred land and is worthy of being respected in that way.

When I say I'm proud to be an American, it's no longer the kind of pride that says we are better than anyone else. It's the kind of pride that says, "Look here, these are honorable people with good intentions that will treat you fairly and will come to your rescue in a crisis." For the most part they wield no more power than ordinary working people do. These are the people I refer to when I say "we the people." I'm proud to be one of them.

I'm saddened to say that the dismal record of behavior left behind by those of us who deal in political power or the power of capital, is almost beyond comprehension. The fact that they represent "we the people" in world affairs is great cause for alarm. The impression they present to the world of who the

American People really are is a false impression. Quite literally the pigs are running the Orwellian Animal Farm. We should all be concerned about that.

During my quiet times in nature, I realized that I was in the presence of a genuine reality that existed before we did and will continue to exist after we are gone. I understand that all of the frantic activity in the towns and cities down below is a manmade creation. I understand that the need to live at a really fast pace is a cultural product born of the need to pay the Vig demanded by the Aristocracy of Capital.

That paradigm is embodied in our image of the modern executive who rises at 5:00 am and is busy working up a sweat on the treadmill, while simultaneously checking the stock ticker, drinking coffee, monitoring his heart rate and catching up on his or her emails. They go on to be besieged by various courtiers who want their attention, only allowing the very most important to have access. Television depicts them as unable to walk from one end of the office to the other without having to sign this very important contract or approve that critical initiative. They delegate to hoards of minions and are urgently needed to play the role of human switchboard. They are handsomely rewarded for doing so. We think they are the ideal humans.

During my thirties, I lived a version of that story as an executive in the shopping center industry. I wanted everything I thought a successful executive should have. At one time or another, I manifested the dream house in the mountains, the boat, the airplane, the travel trailer and the ranchette. None of it made me any happier. Mostly, it just increased my anxiety that I would have to maintain it or that it would all go away. There was a time with hundreds of thousands in the bank, I still felt that anxiety every day. In 1994, I quit and went back to the land.

But, the circumstances of my life have conspired to prevent me from receding into the landscape. It seems there are still battles to fight, both inner and outer. The outer battle is between "we the people" who wish to explore the frontiers of true freedom and the Dominators of the Aristocracy of Capital, who demand that tribute be paid. It's the same battle we fought in 1776.

That battle is still raging today, but it hides behind a great veil of technological deceit. It is not yet time to give up your right and ability to defend yourself. Millions of people lost their homes between 2007 and 2016, as a direct result of the Dominator Agenda. For the most part, they succumbed to their misfortune quietly. After all, if you can't pay your mortgage, you lose your home. That is the law and never mind who caused you to lose your job.

How many millions will have to lose their homes when the next recession comes, before we decide to stand up for our rights? Will it be another 10 million, or 20 million or even 50 million? At some point we will be forced to declare, this is an unjust system and we won't stand for it any more.

The world is still a dangerous place. The danger we face from within our country is at least as potent as the danger we face on the world stage. Jefferson understood that the gradual mutation of the principles upon which our great country was founded may require the people to make a stand for those principles at some time in the future. If you have been fortunate, you may not feel a need to defend yourself yet, but you will certainly feel it if the next Dominator inspired "recession" occurs before we have recovered from the last one. You may be compelled to take a stand.

The inner battle is different. The channels of communication we seem to love so much, whisper in our inner ear:

There is something outside of yourself you must acquire in order to be happy.

We are bombarded with that message every day. It is the cultural belief that has become the **root cause** of our collective malaise. It has formed a stone in our hearts that prevents us from finding our true fulfillment within. It passes sentence upon us and dooms us to a never ending quest to acquire that fulfillment from the material world. That is what it means to look for love in all the wrong places. The pearl of great price is found within.

One of the things that makes me proud to be an American is our commitment to freedom. Freedom walks hand in hand with inspiration and creativity. Over the last two centuries, Americans have demonstrated a natural ability to be both creative and inspired. Those qualities have saved us over and over again from the greatest of perils. Those qualities are an integral part of the American Spirit.

What is the genuine American Spirit? It is a deep yearning to be free to make our own way in pursuit of life, liberty and the right to happiness. It is a deep yearning to be free to enjoy the fruits of our own labors unmolested by politicians, Wall Street pirates or aristocrats. We still have a lot of work to do to secure that freedom.

Nothing less than a re-awakening of the genuine revolutionary American Spirit will save us from Jefferson's Nightmare.

ENDNOTES

1. James B. Glatterfelder, Swiss Federal Institute of Technology, Ownership Networks and Corporate Control: Mapping Economic Power in a Globalized World, 2010.

2. Ricardo Fuentes-Nieva and Nick Galasso, Oxfam Briefing Paper #178, Working for the Few: Political Capture and Economic Inequality, 2014.

3. Ponzi Scheme: A form of fraud in which belief in the success of an enterprise is fostered by the payment of quick returns to early investors from money supplied by later investors. An inherently unstable business venture which fails if growth stops and new investors cannot be found.

4. Mental Floss.com, Ethan Trex, August 2010.

5. The Creature from Jekyll Island 5th Edition by G. Edward Griffin, Copyright 2010, American Media, P.O. Box 4646, Westlake Village, CA 91359

6. Creditsesame.com.

7. Emanuel Saez, UC Berkley, The Evolution of Top Income Gains, Sept. 2013

8. The Economist, Mergers and Antitrust in America, Pushing the Limits, Volume 417, Number 8968, December 12th, 2015.

9. Quantitative Easing: The introduction of new money, created as debt, into the money supply by a central bank.

RECOMMENDED READING

The Great Deformation: The Corruption of Capitalism in America   by David Stockman   Copyright 2013
Public Affairs
250 West 57th St.
New York, NY 10107

The Big Short: Inside the Doomsday Machine
by Michael Lewis   Copyright 2010
W.W. Norton & Company
500 Fifth Avenue
New York, NY 10110

Flashboys: A Wall Street Revolt
by Michael Lewis   Copyright 2014
W.W. Norton & Company
500 Fifth Avenue
New York, NY 10110

Confessions of an Economic Hitman
by John Perkins   Copyright 2004
Penguin Group
375 Hudson Street
New York, NY 10014

The Creature from Jekyll Island 5th Edition
by G. Edward Griffin   Copyright 2010
American Media
P.O. Box 4646
Westlake Village, CA 91359

ABOUT THE AUTHOR

William O. Joseph is a builder, craftsman, inventor, philosopher and public speaker. He is a former Montana state champion target shooter. In company with his wife of 30 years he has spent many years exploring the Rocky Mountains from the back of a horse. These days he likes to spend time exploring Glacier National Park by kayak. He lives and writes in Montana which he feels is truly one of the last best places.

www.ingramcontent.com/pod-product-compliance
Lightning Source LLC
Chambersburg PA
CBHW021046210326
41598CB00016B/1109